CAMBRIDGE LIBRARY COLLECTION

Books of enduring scholarly value

English Men of Letters

In the 1870s, Macmillan publishers began to issue a series of books called 'English Men of Letters' – biographies of English writers by other English writers. The general editor of the series was the journalist, critic, politician, and supporter (and later biographer) of Gladstone, John Morley (1838–1923). The first volume published was *Samuel Johnson*, by Leslie Stephen (1878), and the first series (which continued until 1892) eventually consisted of 39 volumes. The aim was to provide a short introduction to each subject and his works, but also that the life should illuminate the works, and vice versa. All the subjects were men, as were all but one of the authors (Mrs Oliphant on Sheridan); and all but one (Hawthorne) were English or Irish. The subjects range chronologically from Chaucer to Thackeray and Dickens, and an important feature of the series is that many of the authors (Henry James on Hawthorne, Ward on Dickens) were discussing writers of the previous generation, and some (Trollope on Thackeray) had even known their subjects personally. The series exemplifies the British approach to literary biography and criticism at the end of the nineteenth century, and also reveals which authors were at that time regarded as canonical.

Sheridan

The Scots novelist Margaret Oliphant (1828–97) published this biography of the playwright and poet Richard Brinsley Sheridan (1751–1816) in the first 'English Men of Letters' series in 1883. Sheridan is best known for his plays *The Rivals, A Trip to Scarborough,* and *The School for Scandal,* which was his most popular work among his contemporaries. Sheridan was also at one point the owner of the famous Theatre Royal on Drury Lane, which he purchased with his father-in-law in 1776. He led a radical political career, becoming a Whig MP in 1780 and quickly developing a reputation as a brilliant orator. He defended the French Revolution and supported American colonists against British colonial policy. Oliphant's biography covers Sheridan's youth, dramatic writing, political career and middle age; her vivid and sympathetic portrayal provides a valuable insight into his remarkable life.

Cambridge University Press has long been a pioneer in the reissuing of out-of-print titles from its own backlist, producing digital reprints of books that are still sought after by scholars and students but could not be reprinted economically using traditional technology. The Cambridge Library Collection extends this activity to a wider range of books which are still of importance to researchers and professionals, either for the source material they contain, or as landmarks in the history of their academic discipline.

Drawing from the world-renowned collections in the Cambridge University Library, and guided by the advice of experts in each subject area, Cambridge University Press is using state-of-the-art scanning machines in its own Printing House to capture the content of each book selected for inclusion. The files are processed to give a consistently clear, crisp image, and the books finished to the high quality standard for which the Press is recognised around the world. The latest print-on-demand technology ensures that the books will remain available indefinitely, and that orders for single or multiple copies can quickly be supplied.

The Cambridge Library Collection will bring back to life books of enduring scholarly value (including out-of-copyright works originally issued by other publishers) across a wide range of disciplines in the humanities and social sciences and in science and technology.

Sheridan

MARGARET OLIPHANT

CAMBRIDGE
UNIVERSITY PRESS

CAMBRIDGE UNIVERSITY PRESS

Cambridge, New York, Melbourne, Madrid, Cape Town,
Singapore, São Paolo, Delhi, Tokyo, Mexico City

Published in the United States of America by Cambridge University Press, New York

www.cambridge.org
Information on this title: www.cambridge.org/9781108034418

© in this compilation Cambridge University Press 2011

This edition first published 1883
This digitally printed version 2011

ISBN 978-1-108-03441-8 Paperback

English Men of Letters

EDITED BY JOHN MORLEY

SHERIDAN

SHERIDAN

BY

MRS. OLIPHANT

London:

MACMILLAN AND CO.

1883.

NOTE.

THE most important and, on the whole, trustworthy life of Sheridan is that of Moore, published in 1825, nine years after Sheridan's death, and founded upon the fullest information, with the help of all that Sheridan had left behind in the way of papers, and all that the family could furnish—along with Moore's own personal recollections. It is not a very characteristic piece of work, and greatly dissatisfied the friends and lovers of Sheridan; but its authorities are unimpeachable. A previous Memoir by Dr. Watkins, the work of a political opponent and detractor, was without either this kind of authorisation or any grace of personal knowledge, and has fallen into oblivion. Very different is the brief sketch by the well-known Professor Smyth, a most valuable and interesting contribution to the history of Sheridan. It concerns, indeed, only the later part of his life, but it is the most lifelike and, under many aspects, the most touching contemporary portrait that has been made of him. With the professed intention of making up for the absence of character in Moore's *Life*, a small volume of SHERIDANIANA was published the year after, which is full of amusing anecdotes, but little, if any, additional information. Other essays on the subject have been many.

Scarcely an edition of Sheridan's plays has been published (and they are numberless) without a biographical notice, good or bad. The most noted of these is perhaps the *Biographical and Critical Sketch* of Leigh Hunt, which does not, however, pretend to any new light, and is entirely unsympathetic. Much more recently a book of personal *Recollections by an Octogenarian* promised to afford new information ; but, except for the froth of certain dubious and not very savoury stories of the Prince Regent period, failed to do so.

CONTENTS.

RICHARD BRINSLEY SHERIDAN.

CHAPTER I.

HIS YOUTH.

RICHARD BRINSLEY BUTLER SHERIDAN was born in
Dublin, in the month of September 1751, of a family
which had already acquired some little distinction of a
kind quite harmonious with the after fame of him who
made its name so familiar to the world. The Sheridans
were of that Anglo-Irish type which has given so much
instruction and amusement to the world, and which has
indeed in its wit and eccentricity so associated itself with
the fame of its adopted country, that we might almost
say it is from this peculiar variety of the race that we
have all taken our idea of the national character. It
will be a strange thing to discover, after so many years'
identification of the idiosyncrasy as Irish, that in reality
it is a hybrid, and not native to the soil. The race of
brilliant, witty, improvident, and reckless Irishmen whom
we have all been taught to admire, excuse, love, and condemn—the Goldsmiths, the Sheridans, and many more
that will occur to the reader—all belong to this mingled
blood. Many are more Irish, according to our present

S   B

understanding of the word, than their compatriots of a
purer race ; but perhaps it is something of English energy
which has brought them to the front, to the surface,
with an indomitable life which misfortune and the most
reckless defiance of all the laws of living never seem able to
quench. Among these names, and not among the O'Con-
nors and O'Briens, do we find all that is most characteristic,
to modern ideas, in Irish manners and modes of thought.
Nothing more distinct from the Anglo-Saxon type could
be ; and yet it is separated from England in most cases
only by an occasional mixture of Celtic blood—often by
the simple fact of establishment for a few generations on
another soil. How it is that the bog and the mountain,
the softer climate, the salt breath of the Atlantic, should
have wrought this change, is a mystery of Ethnology
which we are quite incompetent to solve ; or whether it
is mere external contact with an influence which the
native gives forth without being himself strongly affected
by it, we cannot tell. But the fact remains that the most
characteristic Irishmen—those through whom we recog-
nise the race—are as a matter of fact, so far as race is
concerned, not Irishmen at all. The same fact tells in
America, where a new type of character seems to have
been ingrafted upon the old by the changed conditions of
so vast a continent and circumstances so peculiar. Even
this, however, is not so remarkable in an altogether new
society, as the absorption, by what was in reality an alien
and a conquering race, of all that is most remarkable in
the national character which they dominated and subdued
—unless indeed we take refuge in the supposition, which
does not seem untenable, that this character, which we
have been so hasty in identifying with it, is not really

Irish at all; and that we have not yet fathomed the
natural spirit, overlaid by such a *couche* of superficial
foreign brilliancy, of that more mystic race, full of tragic
elements, of visionary faith and purity, of wild revenge
and subtle cunning, which is in reality native to the old
island of the saints. Certainly the race of Columba seems
to have little in common with the race of Sheridan.

The two immediate predecessors of the great dramatist
are both highly characteristic figures, and thoroughly
authentic, which is as much perhaps as any man of letters
need care for. The first of these, Dr. Thomas Sheridan,
Brinsley Sheridan's grandfather, was a clergyman and
schoolmaster in Dublin in the early part of the eighteenth
century—by all reports an excellent scholar and able
instructor, but extravagant and hot-headed after his
kind. He was the intimate friend aud associate of
Swift in his later years, and lent a little brightness to
the great Dean's society when he returned disappointed
to his Irish preferment. Lord Orrery describes this
genial but reckless parson in terms which are entirely
harmonious with the after development of the family
character :—

" He had that kind of good nature which absence of mind,
indolence of body, and carelessness of fortune produce ; and
although not over-strict in his own conduct, yet he took care
of the morality of his scholars, whom he sent to the university remarkably well-grounded in all kinds of learning, and not
ill-instructed in the social duties of life. He was slovenly,
indigent, and cheerful. He knew books better than men, and
he knew the value of money least of all."

The chief point in Dr. Sheridan's career is of a tragi-
comic character which still further increases the appro-

priateness of his appearance at the head of his descendants.
By Swift's influence he was appointed to a living in Cork,
in addition to which he was made one of the Lord-
Lieutenant's chaplains, and thus put in the way of
promotion generally. But on one unlucky Sunday the
following incident occurred. It must be remembered
that these were the early days of the Hanoverian succession, and that Ireland had been the scene of the last
struggle for the Stuarts. He was preaching in Cork, in
the principal church of the town on the 1st of August,
which was kept as the King's birthday.

"Dr. Sheridan, after a very solemn preparation, and when
he had drawn to himself the mute attention of his congregation, slowly and emphatically delivered his text, *Sufficient
unto the day is the evil thereof.* The congregation being
divided in political opinions, gave to the text a decided
political construction, and on the reverend preacher again
reading the text with more marked emphasis became excited,
and listened to the sermon with considerable restlessness and
anxiety."

Another account describes this sermon as having been
preached before the Lord-Lieutenant himself, an honour
for which the preacher was not prepared, and which
confused him so much that he snatched up the first sermon that came to hand, innocent of all political intention,
as well as of the date which gave such piquancy to his
text. But whatever the cause, the effect was disastrous.
He "shot his fortune dead by chance-medley" with this
single text. He lost his chaplaincy, and is even said to
have been forbidden the viceregal court, and all the ways
of promotion were closed to him for ever. But his spirit
was not broken by his evil luck. "Still he remained a
punster, a quibbler, a fiddler, and a wit. Not a day

passed without a rebus, an anagram, or a madrigal. His
pen and his fiddle were constantly in motion." He had
"such a ready wit and flow of humour that it was impossible for any, even the most splenetic man not to be
cheerful in his company." "In the invitations sent to
the Dean, Sheridan was always included; nor was Swift
to be seen in perfect good humour unless when he made
part of the company." Nothing could be more congenial to the name of Sheridan than the description of
this lighthearted and easy-minded clerical humorist,
whose wit no doubt flashed like lightning about all the
follies of the mimic court which had cast him out, and
whose jovial hand-to-mouth existence had all that acci-
dentalness and mixture of extravagance and penury
which is the natural atmosphere of such reckless souls.
It is even said that Swift made use of his abilities and
appropriated his wit: the reader must judge for himself whether the Dean had any need of thieving in that
particular.

Dr. Sheridan's son, Thomas Sheridan, was a very
different man. He was very young when he was left to
make his way in the world for himself; he had been
designed, it would appear, to be a schoolmaster like his
father; but the stage has always had an attraction for
those whose associations are connected with that more
serious stage, the pulpit, and Thomas Sheridan became
an actor. He is the author of a life of Swift, said to
be "pompous and dull,"—qualities which seem to have
mingled oddly in his own character with the lighthearted
recklessness of his race. His success on the stage was
not so great as was his popularity as a teacher of elocution, an art for which he seems to have conceived an

almost fanatical enthusiasm. Considering oratory, not
without reason, as the master of all arts, he spent a great
part of his life in eager efforts to form a school for its
study, after a method of his own. This was not a successful project, nor, according to the little gleam of light
thrown upon his system by Dr. Parr, does it seem to
have been a very elevated one. "One of Richard's
sisters now and then visited Harrow," he says, "and well
do I remember that in the house where I lodged she
triumphantly repeated Dryden's ode upon St. Cecilia's
Day, according to the instruction given her by her father.
Take a sample :—

> ' *None* but the brave,
> None but the *brave,*
> None *but* the brave deserve the fair.' "

Thomas Sheridan, however, was not without appreciation as an actor, and, like every ambitious player of the
time, had his hopes of rivalling Garrick, and was fondly
considered by his friends to be worthy comparison with
that king of actors. He married a lady who held no
inconsiderable place in the light literature of the time,
which was little, as yet, invaded by feminine adventure—
the author of a novel called *Sidney Biddulph* and of various
plays.   And there is a certain reflection of the same kind
of friendship which existed between Swift and the elder
Sheridan in Boswell's description, in his *Life of Johnson,*
of the loss his great friend had sustained through a
quarrel with Thomas Sheridan " of one of his most agreeable resources for amusement in his lonely evenings."
It would appear that at this time (1763) Sheridan and
his wife were settled in London.

" Sheridan's well-informed, animated, and bustling mind
never suffered conversation to stagnate," Boswell adds, "and
Mrs. Sheridan was a most agreeable companion to an intellectual man.   She was sensible, ingenious, unassuming, yet
communicative.   I recollect with satisfaction many pleasing
hours which I passed with her under the hospitable roof of
her husband, who was to me a very kind friend.   Her novel
entitled *Memoirs of Miss Sidney Biddulph* contains an excellent
moral, while it inculcates a future state of retribution ; and
what it teaches is impressed upon the mind by a series of as
deep distresses as can afflict humanity in the amiable and
pious heroine. . . . Johnson paid her this high compliment
upon it : 'I know not, madam, that you have a right upon
high principles to make your readers suffer so much.'"

The cause of Johnson's quarrel with Sheridan is said
to have been some slighting words reported to the latter,
which Johnson had let fall when he heard that Sheridan
had received a pension of £200 a year from Government.
"What ! have they given *him* a pension ? then it is time
for me to give up mine "—a not unnatural cause of
offence, and all the more so that Sheridan flattered himself he had, by his interest with certain members of the
ministry, who had been his pupils, helped to procure his
pension for Johnson himself.

These were the palmy days of the Sheridan family.
Their children, of whom Richard was the third, had been
born in Dublin, where the two little boys, Richard and
his elder brother Charles, began their education under the
charge of a schoolmaster named Whyte, to whom they
were committed with a despairing letter from their
mother, who evidently had found the task of their education too much for her.   Perhaps Mrs. Sheridan, in an age
of epigrams, was not above the pleasure, so seductive to
all who possess the gift, of writing a clever letter.   She

tells the schoolmaster that the little pupils she is sending
him will be his tutors in the excellent quality of patience.
"I have hitherto been their only instructor," she says,
" and they have sufficiently exercised mine, for two such
impenetrable dunces I never met with." This is the
first certificate with which the future wit and dramatist
appeared before the world. When the parents went to
London in 1762, the boys naturally accompanied them.
And this being a time of prosperity, when Thomas
Sheridan had Cabinet Ministers for his pupils, and interest enough to help the great man of letters of the age
to a pension, it is not to be wondered if that hope which
never springs eternal in any human breast so warmly as
in that of a man who lives by his wits, and never knows
what the morrow may bring forth, should have so
encouraged the vivacious Irishman as to induce him to
send his boys to Harrow, proud to give them the best of
education, and opportunity of making friends for themselves. His pension, his pupils, his acting, his wife's
literary gains, all conjoined to give a promise of prosperity. When his friends discussed him behind his
back, it is true they were not very favourable to him.
"There is to be seen in Sheridan something to reprehend,
and everything to laugh at," says Johnson, in his "big
bow-wow style;" "but, sir, he is not a bad man. No,
sir : were mankind to be divided into good and bad, he
would stand considerably within the ranks of the good."
The same authority said of him that though he could
" exhibit no character," yet he excelled in "plain declamation"; and he was evidently received in very good
society, and was hospitable and entertained his friends,
as it was his nature to do. Evidently, too, he had no

small opinion of himself. It is from Johnson's own mouth that the following anecdote at once of his liberality and presumption is derived. It does not show his critic, perhaps, in a more favourable light.

"Sheridan is a wonderful admirer of the tragedy of *Douglas*, and presented its author with a gold medal. Some years ago, at a coffee-house in Oxford, I called to him—'Mr. Sheridan, Mr. Sheridan! how came you to give a gold medal to Home for writing that horrid play?' This you see was wanton and insolent : but I meant to be wanton and insolent. A medal has no value but as a stamp of merit, and was Sheridan to assume to himself the right of giving that stamp? If Sheridan was magnificent enough to bestow a gold medal as an honorary mark of dramatic merit, he should have requested one of the Universities to choose the person on whom it should be conferred. Sheridan had no right to give a stamp of merit ; it was counterfeiting Apollo's coin."

The Irishman's vanity, prodigality, and hasty assumption of an importance to which he had no right could scarcely be better exemplified—nor, perhaps, the reader will say, the privileged arrogance of the great critic. It is more easy to condone the careless extravagance of the one than the deliberate insolence of the other. The comment, however, is just enough ; and so, perhaps, was his description of the Irishman's attempt to improve the elocution of his contemporaries. "What influence can Mr. Sheridan have upon the language of this great country by his narrow exertions?" asks the great lexicographer. "Sir, it is burning a candle at Dover to show light at Calais." But when Johnson says, "Sir, Sherry is dull, naturally dull : but it must have taken him a great deal of pains to become what we now see him. Such an excess of stupidity, sir, is not in nature,"—we acknow-

ledge the wit, but doubt the fact. Thomas Sheridan very
likely wanted humour, and was unable to perceive when
he made himself ridiculous, as in the case of the medal;
but we want a great deal more evidence to induce us to
believe that the son of the jovial Dublin priest, and the
father of Sheridan the great, could have been dull. He
was very busy—"bustling," as Boswell calls him, his
schemes going to his head, his vanity and enthusiasm
combined making him feel himself an unappreciated
reformer—a prophet thrown away upon an ungrateful
age. But stupidity had nothing to do with his follies.
He was "a wrong-headed whimsical man," Dr. Parr tells
us, but adds, "I respected him, and he really liked me
and did me some important services." "I once or twice
met his (Richard Sheridan's) mother: she was quite celes-
tial." Such are the testimonies of their contemporaries.

It was not long, however, that the pair were able to
remain in London. There is a whimsical indication of
the state of distress into which Thomas Sheridan soon
fell in the mention by Boswell of "the extraordinary
attention in his own country" with which he had been
"honoured," by having had "an exception made in his
favour in an Irish Act of Parliament concerning insolvent
debtors." "Thus to be singled out," says Johnson, "by
Legislature as an object of public consideration and
kindness is a proof of no common merit." It was a
melancholy kind of proof, however, and one which few
would choose to be gratified by. The family went to
France, leaving their boys at Harrow, scraping together
apparently as much as would pay their expenses there—
no small burden upon a struggling man. And at Blois,
in 1766, Mrs. Sheridan died. "She appears," says Moore,

"to have been one of those rare women who, united
to men of more pretensions but less real intellect than
themselves, meekly conceal this superiority even from
their own hearts, and pass their lives without a remonstrance or murmur in gently endeavouring to repair those
evils which the indiscretion or vanity of their partners
have brought upon them." Except that she found him
at seven an impenetrable dunce, there is no record of
any tie of sympathy existing between Mrs. Sheridan
and her brilliant boy.

He had not perhaps, indeed, ever appeared in this
character during his mother's lifetime. At Harrow he
made but an unsatisfactory appearance. " There was
little in his boyhood worth communication," says Dr.
Parr, whose long letter on the subject all Sheridan's
biographers quote; "he was inferior to many of his
schoolfellows in the ordinary business of a school, and I
do not remember any one instance in which he distinguished himself by Latin or English composition
either in prose or verse." This is curious enough; but
it is not impossible that the wayward boy, if he did
adventure himself in verse, would think it best to keep
his youthful compositions sacred from a master's eye.
Verse writers, both in the dead languages and in the
living, flourished at Harrow in those days of whom no
one has heard since, " but Richard Sheridan aspired to
no rivalry with either of them." Notwithstanding this
absence of all the outward show of talent, Parr was not
a man to remain unconscious of the glimmer of genius in
the Irish boy's bright eyes. When he found that Dick
would not construe as he ought, he laid plans to take him
with craft, and " did not fail to probe and tease him."

"I stated his case with great good humour to the upper master, who was one of the best tempered men in the world : and it was agreed between us that Richard should be called oftener and worked more severely. The varlet was not suffered to stand up in his place, but was summoned to take his station near the master's table, where the voice of no prompter could reach him : and in this defenceless condition he was so harassed that he at last gathered up some grammatical rules and prepared himself for his lessons. While this tormenting process was inflicted upon him, I now and then upbraided him. But you will take notice that he did not incur any corporal punishment for his idleness : his industry was just sufficient to keep him from disgrace. All the while Sumner and I saw in him vestiges of a superior intellect. His eye, his countenance, his general manner, were striking ; his answers to any common question were prompt and acute. We knew the esteem and even admiration which somehow or other all his schoolfellows felt for him. He was mischievous enough, but his pranks were accompanied by a sort of vivacity and cheerfulness which delighted Sumner and myself. I had much talk with him about his apple loft, for the supply of which all the gardens in the neighbourhood were taxed, and some of the lower boys were employed to furnish it. I threatened, but without asperity, to trace the depredators through his associates up to the leader. He with perfect good humour set me at defiance, and I never could bring home the charge to him. All boys and all masters were pleased with him."

The amount of "good humour" in this sketch is enough to make the Harrow of last century look like a scholastic paradise ; and the humorous torture to which young Sheridan was subjected shows a high sense of the appropriate either in "the best tempered man in the world," or in the learned doctor who loved to set forth his own doings and judgment in the best light, and had the advantage of telling his story after events had shown what the pupil was. Parr, however, modestly

disowns the credit of having developed the intellectual powers of Sheridan, and neither were they stimu-
lated into literary effort by Sumner, the head-master of
Harrow, who was a friend of his father, and had therefore additional opportunities of knowing the boy's capabilities. " We both of us discovered great talents which
neither of us were capable of calling into action while
Sheridan was a schoolboy," Parr says.   In short, it is
evident that the boy, always popular and pleasant,
amusing and attracting his schoolfellows, and on perfectly amicable terms with the masters, even when he
was doubtful about his lesson, took no trouble whatever with his work, and cared nothing for the honours
of school.   He kept himself afloat, and that was all.
His sins were not grievous in any way.   He had it not
in his power to be extravagant, for Thomas Sheridan in
his bankrupt condition must have had hard enough ado
to keep his boys at Harrow at all.   But it is very clear
that neither scholarship nor laborious mental exertion
of any kind tempted him.   He took the world lightly
and gaily, and enjoyed his schoolboy years all the more
that there was nothing of the struggle of young ambition
in them.   When his family came back from France
shortly after the mother's death, it is with a little gush
of enthusiasm that his sister describes her first meeting after long separation with the delightful brother
whom she had half forgotten, and who appears like a
young hero in all the early bloom of seventeen, with
his Irish charm and his Harrow breeding, to the eyes of
the little girl, accustomed no doubt to shabby enough
gentlemen in the cheap retreats of English poverty in
France.

" He was handsome, not merely in the eyes of a partial
sister, but generally allowed to be so.   His cheeks had the
glow of health, his eyes—the finest in the world—the brilliancy of genius, and were soft as a tender and affectionate
heart could render them.   The same playful fancy, the same
sterling and innoxious wit that was shown afterwards in his
writings, cheered and delighted the family circle.   I admired
—I almost adored him ! "

No doubt the handsome merry boy was a delightful
novelty in the struggling family,where even the girls were
taught to mouth verses, and the elder brother had begun
to accompany his father on his half-vagabond career as a
lecturer, to give examples of the system of elocution
upon which he had concentrated all his faculties.   After
a short stay in London the family went to Bath, where
for a time they settled, the place in its high days of
fashion being propitious to all the arts.   The father,
seldom at home, lived a hard enough life, lecturing,
teaching, sometimes playing, pursuing his favourite object
as hotly as was practicable through all the struggles
necessary to get a living, such as it was, now abundant,
now meagre, for his family ; while the girls and boys
lived a sort of hap-hazard existence in the gay city,
getting what amusement they could—motherless, and
left to their own resources, yet finding society of a sufficiently exciting kind among the visitors with whom the
town overflowed, and the artist-folk who entertained
them.   Here, while Charles worked with his father,
Richard would seem to have done nothing at all, but
doubtless strolled about the fashionable promenade among
the bucks and beaux, and heard all that was going on,
and saw the scandal-makers nod their heads together,
and the officers now and then arrange a duel, and Lydia

Languish ransack the circulating libraries. They were
all about in those lively streets, Mrs. Malaprop deranging
her epitaphs, and Sir Lucius with his pistols always
ready, and the little waiting-maid tripping about the
scene with Delia's letters and *Broken Vows* under her
arm. The young gentleman swaggering among them saw
everything without knowing it, and remembered those
familiar figures when the time came : but in the meanwhile did nothing, living pleasantly with his young sisters,
no doubt very kind to them, and spending all the money
the girls could spare out of their little housekeeping,
and falling in love, the most natural amusement of all.

It is wrong, however, to say that he was entirely
idle.   At Harrow he had formed an intimate friendship with a youth more ambitious than himself, the
Nathaniel Halhed whom Dr. Parr chronicles as having
" written well in Latin and Greek." With this young
man Sheridan entered into a sort of literary partnership
both in classical translation and dramatic composition.
Their first attempt was a farce called *Jupiter ;* the
subject being the story of Ixion, in which, curiously
enough, the after-treatment of the *Critic* is shadowed
forth in various points, the little drama being in the
form of a rehearsal before a tribunal not unlike that to
which Mr. Puff submits his immortal tragedy.   Simile,
the supposed author, indeed says one or two things which
are scarcely unworthy of Puff.   The following passage
occurs in a scene in which he is explaining to his critics
the new fashion of composition, how the music is made
first, and "the sense" afterwards (a process no ways
astonishing to the present generation), and how "a complete set of scenes from Italy" is the first framework of

the play which "some ingenious hand" writes up to. "By this method," says one of the wondering commentators, " you must often commit blunders ? "

"*Simile.* Blunders ! to be sure I must, but I always could get myself out of them again. Why, I'll tell you an instance of it. You must know I was once a journeyman sonnet-writer to Signor Squaltini. Now, his method, when seized with the *furor harmonicus*, was constantly to make me sit by his side, while he was thrumming on his harpsichord, in order to make extempore verses to whatever air he should beat out to his liking. I remember one morning as he was in this situation—*thrum, thrum, thrum* (moving his fingers as if beating on the harpsichord), striking out something prodigiously great as he thought—'Hah !' said he ; 'hah ! Mr. Simile—*thrum, thrum, thrum*—by gar, him is vary fine—write me some words directly.' I durst not interrupt him to ask on what subject, so instantly began to describe a fine morning.

> Calm was the land and calm the skies,
> And calm the heaven's dome serene,
> Hush'd was the gale and hush'd the breeze,
> And not a vapour to be seen.

I sang it to his notes. ' Hah ! upon my word, vary pritt—*thrum, thrum, thrum.* Stay, stay ! Now, upon my word, here it must be an adagio. *Thrum, thrum, thrum.* Oh ! let it be an Ode to Melancholy.'
Monop. The devil ! then you were puzzled sure——
Sim. Not in the least ! I brought in a cloud in the next stanza, and matters, you see, came about at once.
Monop. An excellent transition.
O'Cd. Vastly ingenious, indeed.
Sim. Was it not, very ? it required a little command—a little presence of mind."

When the rehearsal begins, the resemblance is still more perfect, though there is no reproduction either of the plot or characters introduced. We are not told how much share Halhed had in the composition : it was he

who furnished the skeleton of the play, but it is scarcely
possible that such a scene as the above could be from
any hand but Sheridan's. This youthful effort was never
finished. It was to have brought in a sum of money,
which they both wanted much, to the young authors :
"The thoughts," Halhed says, "of £200 shared between
us are enough to bring the water into one's eyes." Halhed, then at Oxford, wanted the money above all things
to enable him to pay a visit to Bath, where lived the
young lady whom all these young men adored ; and young
Sheridan, who can doubt, required it for a thousand uses.
But they were both at an age when a great part of pleasure lies in the planning, and when the mind is easily
diverted to another and another new beginning. A publication of the *Tatler* type was the next project, to be
called (one does not know why) *Hernan's Miscellany ;*
but this never went further than a part composition of
the first number, which is somewhat feeble and flippant, as
the monologue of an essayist of that old-fashioned type, if
not under any special inspiration, is apt to be. Finally
the young men succeeded in producing a volume of so-
called translations from a dubious Latin author called
Aristænetus, of whom no one knows much, and on whom
at least it was very easy for them to father the light and
frothy verses, which no one was likely to seek for in the
original—if an original existed. Their preface favours the
idea that the whole business was a literary hoax by which
they did not even expect their readers to be taken in.
Aristænetus got itself published, the age being fond of
classics rubbed down into modern verse, but does not seem
to have done any more. The two young men were in hopes
that Sumner, their old master, " and the wise few of their

acquaintance," would talk about the book, and perhaps discover the joint authorship, and help them to fame and profit. But these hopes were not realised, as indeed they did not in the least deserve to be. They were flattered by being told that Johnson was supposed to be the author, which must have been a friendly invention; and Halhed tried to believe that " everybody had read the book," and that the second part, vaguely promised in the preface on condition of the success of the first, " should be published immediately, being of opinion that the readers of the first volume would be sure to purchase the second, and that the publication of the second would put it into the heads of others to buy the first,"—a truly business-like argument, which, however, did not convince the book-sellers. It seems a pity to burden the collection of Sheridan's works now with these unprofitable verses, which were never acknowledged, and did not even procure for young Halhed, who wanted it so much, the happiness of a visit to Bath, or a sight of the object of his boyish adoration.

It is the presence of this lady which gives interest and romance to the early chapter of Sheridan's life, and the record cannot go further without bringing her in. There flourished at Bath in those days a family called by Dr. Burney, in his *History of Music*, a nest of nightingales, —the family of Linley, the composer, who had been for years at the head of musical enterprise in the district, the favourite singing master, the conductor of all the concerts, a man whom Bath delighted to honour, and whose fame spread over England by means of the *beau monde* which took the waters in that city of pleasure. The position that such a man takes in a provincial town has become once more so much like what it was in the latter half of

last century, when Handel was at Windsor and England in one of its musical periods, that it will be easily
realised by the reader. The brevet rank, revocable at
the pleasure of society, which the musical family obtains,
its admission among all the fine people, the price it has to
pay for its elevation, and the vain hope that it is prized
for its own personal qualities, which flatters it while in its
prime of attraction,—the apparent equality, nay, almost
superiority, of the triumphant musicians among their patrons, who yet never forget the real difference between
them, and whose homage is often little more than a form of
insult,—give a dramatic interest to the group such as few
possess. This was the position held by the Linleys among
the fine people of Bath. There were beautiful girls in
the musician's house, which was always open, hospitable,
and bright, and where a perpetual flutter of admiration
and compliments, half affectionate, half humorous, the
enthusiasm of a coterie, was in the ears of the young creatures in all their early essays in art. Men of wealth and
sometimes of rank, the gentlemen of the neighbourhood,
the officers and the wits,—all friends of Linley, and glad
to invite him to club and coffee-house and mess-room,—
were always about to furnish escorts and a flattering train
wherever the young singers went. The eldest daughter,
Elizabeth—or Eliza, as it was the fashion of the time
to shorten and vulgarise that beautiful name—was a
lovely girl of sixteen when the young Sheridans became
known about Bath. Her voice was as lovely as her face,
and she was the prima donna of her father's concerts,
going with him to sing at festivals in other cathedral
towns, and often to Oxford, where she had turned the
head of young Halhed and of many an undergraduate

beside.   In Bath the young men were all at her feet, and
not only the young men, as was natural, but the elder and
less innocent members of society.   That the musician and
his wife might have entertained hopes or even allowed
themselves to be betrayed into not entirely unjustifiable
schemings to marry their beautiful child to somebody who
would raise her into a higher sphere, may well be believed.
One such plan indeed it is evident did exist, which the
poor girl herself foiled by making an artless confession
to the man whom her parents had determined she should
marry — " Mr. Long, an old gentleman of considerable
fortune," who had the magnanimity to take upon himself
the burden of breaking the engagement, and closed the
indignant father's mouth by settling a little fortune of
£3000 upon the young lady.

A danger escaped in this way, however, points to many
other pitfalls among which her young feet had to tread,
and one at least of a far more alarming kind has secured
for itself a lasting place in her future husband's history.
There is a curious letter [1] extant, which is printed in all
Sheridan's biographies, and in which Eliza gives an account to a dear friend and confidant of the toils woven
around her by one of her father's visitors, a certain
Captain Matthews, who, though a married man and much
older than herself, had beguiled the simple girl into a
prolonged and clandestine sentimental correspondence.
The sophisticated reader, glancing at this quaint production, without thought of the circumstances or the

---

[1] Mrs. Norton in a preliminary sketch to an intended history of
the Sheridans, never written, denies the authenticity of this letter
with a somewhat ill-directed family pride : but no doubt has been
thrown upon it by any of Sheridan's biographers.

person, would probably conclude that there was harm in
it, which it is very certain from all that is said and done
besides did not exist; but the girl in her innocence evidently felt that the stolen intercourse, the whisperings
aside, the man's protestations of fondness, and despair if
she withdrew from him, and her own half-flattered half-
frightened attraction towards him, were positive guilt.
The letter, indeed, is Lydia Languish from beginning to
end,—the Lydia Languish of real life without any genius
to trim her utterance into just as much as is needful and
characteristic,—and in consequence is somewhat tedious,
long-winded, and confused; but her style, something
between Clarissa Harlowe and Julia Mannering, is quite
appropriate at once to the revelation and the period.
The affair to which her letter refers has occupied far too
much space, we think, in the story of Sheridan's life, yet
it is a curious exposition of the time, the class, and the
locality.   The Maid of Bath, as she was called, had
many adorers.   Young Halhed, young Charles Sheridan
—neither of them with much to offer—followed her
steps wherever she moved, and applauded to the echo
every note she sang, as did many another adorer; while
within the busy and full house the middle-aged visitor,
her father's so-called friend, had a hundred opportunities
for a whispered word, a stolen caress, half permissible for
the sake of old friendship, and because no doubt he had
known her from a child.   But even at sixteen the eyes
of a girl accustomed to so many tributes would soon be
opened, and the poor Lydia became alarmed by the
warmth of her half-paternal lover and by the secrecy of
his communications.   This was her position at the time
the Sheridans appear upon the scene.

The new influence immediately began to tell. Miss Linley and Miss Sheridan became devoted friends—and the two brothers "on our first acquaintance both professed to love me." She gave them no hope "that I should ever look upon them in any other light than as brothers of my friend;" but yet "preferred the youngest" as "by far the most agreeable in person, beloved by every one, and greatly respected by all the better sort of people." Richard Sheridan, it would seem, immediately assumed the position of the young lady's secret guardian. He made friends with Matthews, became even intimate with him, and thus discovered the villainous designs which he entertained; while, on the other hand, he obtained the confidence of the lady, and became her chief adviser. It was a curious position for a young man—but he was very young, very poor, without any prospects that could justify him in entering the lists on his own account; and while he probably succeeded in convincing Miss Linley that his love for her was subdued into friendship, he seems to have been able to keep his secret from all his competitors, and not to have been suspected by any of them. In the heat of the persecution by Matthews, who resisted all her attempts to shake off his society, frightening her by such old-fashioned expedients as threatening his own life, and declaring that he could not live without seeing her—incessant consultations were necessary with the young champion who knew the secret, and whose advice and countenance were continually appealed to. No doubt they met daily in the ordinary course at each other's houses; but romance made it desirable that they should find a secret spot where Eliza could confide her troubles to Richard, and he warn her and encourage her in her

resistance. "A grotto in Sydney Gardens" is reported
to have been the scene of these meetings. On one occasion the anxious adviser must have urged his warnings
too far, or insisted too warmly upon the danger of her
position, for she left him angrily, resenting his interference : and this was the occasion of the verses addressed
to Delia which he left upon the seat of the grotto for her,
with an apparently well-justified but somewhat rash confidence that they would fall into no other hands. In
this, after celebrating the "moss-covered grotto of stone"
and the dew-dripping willow that overshadows it, he
unfolds the situation as follows :—

> " —this is the grotto where Delia reclined,
>   As late I in secret her confidence sought ;
> And this is the tree kept her safe from the wind,
>   As blushing she heard the grave lesson I taught.
>
> " Then tell me thou grotto of moss-covered stone,
>   And tell me thou willow with leaves dripping dew,
> Did Delia seem vexed when Horatio was gone,
>   And did she confess her resentment to you ?
>
> " Methinks now each bough as you're waving it tries
>   To whisper a cause for the sorrow I feel,
> To hint how she frowned when I dared to advise,
>   And sigh'd when she saw that I did it with zeal.
>
> " True, true, silly leaves, so she did I allow ;
>   She frowned, but no rage in her looks did I see ;
> She frowned, but reflection had clouded her brow,
>   She sigh'd, but perhaps 'twas in pity for me.
>
> .   .   .   .   .   .
>
> " For well did she know that my heart meant no wrong,
>   It sank at the thought but of giving her pain ;
> But trusted its task to a faltering tongue,
>   Which err'd from the feelings it would not explain.

" Yet oh, if indeed I've offended the maid,
    If Delia my humble monition refuse,—
Sweet willow, the next time she visits thy shade,
    Fan gently her bosom and plead its excuse.

" And thou, stony grot, in thy arch may'st preserve
    Two lingering drops of the night-fallen dew ;
And just let them fall at her feet, and they'll serve
    As tears of my sorrow entrusted to you."

This is not very fine poetry ; but it is very instructive
as to the curious complication of affairs. It would not
have suited Captain Absolute to play such a part ; but
Lydia Languish, amid all the real seriousness of the
dilemma, no doubt would have derived a certain comfort
from the romantic circumstances altogether—the villain,
on one hand, threatening to lay his death at her door ;
the modest self-suppressed adorer, on the other, devoting
himself to her service ; the long confidential conferences
in the dark and damp little shelter behind the willow ;
the verses left on the seat ;—nothing could have been
more delightful to a romantic imagination.

But the excitement heightened as time went on ; and
the poor girl was so harassed and persecuted by the man
whose suit was a scandal, that she tried at last, she tells us,
to take poison as the only way of escape for her, searching
for and finding in Miss Sheridan's room a small phial of
laudanum, which had been used for an aching tooth, and
which was too small apparently to do any harm. After
this tremendous evidence of her miserable state, Sheridan,
who would seem to have confined himself hitherto to
warnings and hints, now disclosed the full turpitude of
Matthews' intentions, and showed her a letter in which
the villain announced that he had determined to proceed

to strong measures, and if he could not overcome her by
pleadings meant to carry her off by force.   " The moment
I read this horrid letter I fainted, and it was some time
before I could recover my senses sufficiently to thank Mr.
Sheridan for opening my eyes." But the question now
was, What was to be done? For the poor girl seems to
have had no confidence in her father's power of protecting her, and probably knew the inexpediency of embroil-
ing him with his patrons. The two young creatures laid
their foolish heads together in this crisis of fate—the
girl thoroughly frightened, the youth full of chivalrous
determination to protect her, and doubtless not without
a hotheaded young lover's hope to turn it to his own
advantage. He proposed that she should fly to France,
and there take refuge in a convent till the danger should
be over. His own family had left France only a few
years before, and the sister who was Eliza's friend would
recommend her to the kind nuns at St. Quentin, where
she had herself been brought up. "He would go with
me to protect me, and after he had seen me settled he
would return to England and place my conduct in such
a light that the world would applaud and not condemn
me."

Such was the wonderful expedient by which the difficulties of this terrible crisis were surmounted. Her
mother was ill and the house in great disorder, and under
cover of the accidental commotion young Sheridan
handed the agitated girl into a chair,—his sister, who
was in the secret, and, no doubt, in high excitement too,
coming secretly to help her to pack up her clothes ; and
that night they posted off to London. "Sheridan had
engaged the wife of one of his servants to go with me as

a maid without my knowledge. You may imagine how
pleased I was with his delicate behaviour." This last
particular reaches the very heights of chivalry, for, no
doubt, it must have been quite a different matter to the
impassioned boy to conduct the flight, with a commonplace matron seated in his post-chaise between him and
his beautiful Delia, instead of the *tête-à-tête* which he might
so easily have secured. Next day they crossed the Channel
to the little sandy port of Dunkirk and were safe.

And it would seem that the rash young lover was
very honest and really meant to carry out this mad
project; for she did eventually reach her convent, whither
he attended her with punctilious respect. But when
they were fairly launched upon their adventurous career,
either common sense or discreet acquaintances soon made
it apparent to the young man that a youth and a maiden,
however virtuous, cannot rove about the world in this way
without comment, and that there was but one thing to
be done in the circumstances. Perhaps Miss Linley had
begun to feel something more than the mere " preference
for the youngest," which she had so calmly announced,
or perhaps it was only the desperate nature of the circumstances that made her yield. But however that may
be, the two fugitives went through the ceremony of marriage at Calais, though they seem to have separated
immediately afterwards, carrying out the high sentimental
and Platonic romance to the end.

It is a curious commentary, however, upon the prodigality of the penniless class to which Sheridan belonged,
that he could manage to start off suddenly upon this
journey out of Thomas Sheridan's shifty household, where
money was never abundant, a boy of twenty with nothing

of his own—hurrying up to London with post-horses, and hiring magnificently " the wife of one of his servants " to attend upon his love. The words suggest a retinue of retainers, and the journey itself would have taxed the resources of a youth much better endowed than Sheridan. Did he borrow, or run chivalrously into debt? or how did he manage it? His sister " assisted them with money out of her little fund for house expenses," but that would not go far. Perhaps the friend in London (a " respectable brandy-merchant") to whom he introduced Miss Linley as an heiress who had eloped with him, may have helped on such a warrant to furnish the funds. But there is nothing more remarkable than the ease with which these impecunious gallants procure post-chaises, servants, and luxuries in those dashing days. The young men think nothing of a headlong journey from Bath to London and back again, which, notwithstanding all our increased facilities of locomotion, penniless youths of to-day would hesitate about. To be sure it is possible that credit was to be had at the livery-stables, whereas, fortunately, none is possible at the railway station. Post-horses seem to have been an affair of every day to the heroes of the Crescent and the Parade.

Meanwhile everything was left in commotion at home. Charles Sheridan, the elder brother, had left Bath and gone to the country in such dejection, after Miss Linley's final refusal of his addresses, as became a sentimental lover. When Richard went off triumphant with the lady, his sisters were left alone in great excitement and agitation, and their landlord, thinking the girls required "protection," according to the language of the time, set out at break of day to bring back the rejected from his retirement. The feelings of Charles on finding that his younger brother, whom even the girls did not know to be a lover of Miss Linley, had carried off the prize, may be imagined. But the occasion of the elopement, the designing villain of the piece,—the profligate whose pursuit had driven the lady to despair,—was furious. Miss Linley had no doubt left some explanation of the extraordinary step she was taking with her parents, and Sheridan appears to have taken the same precaution and disclosed the reasons which prompted her flight. When Matthews heard of this he published the following advertisement in a Bath newspaper.

"Mr. Richard S * * * * * * * having attempted, in a letter left behind him for that purpose, to account for his scandalous method of running away from this place by insinuations derogatory to *my* character and that of a young lady innocent so far as relates to *me* or *my* knowledge ; since which he has neither taken any notice of letters, or even informed his own family of the place where he has hid himself: I can no longer think he deserves the treatment of a gentleman, and therefore shall trouble myself no further about him than, in this public method, to post him as a L * * * and a treacherous S * * * * * * * *

"And as I am convinced there have been many malevolent incendiaries concerned in the propagation of this infamous lie, if any of them, unprotected by age, infirmities, or profession, will dare to acknowledge the part they have acted, and affirm *to* what they have said *of* me, they may depend on receiving the proper reward of their villainy in the most public manner."

This fire-eating paragraph was signed with the writer's name, and it may be imagined what a delightful commotion it made in such a metropolis of scandal and leisure, and with what excitement all the frequenters of the

pump-room and the assemblies looked for the next incident. Some weeks elapsed before they were satisfied,
but the following event was striking enough to content the
most sensational imagination. It would seem to have
been April before a clue was found to the fugitives, and
Linley started at once from Bath to recover his daughter.
He found her, to his great relief doubtless, in the house
of an English doctor in Lisle, who had brought her there
from her convent, and placed her under his wife's care
to be nursed when she was ill. Everything, it was
evident, had been done in honour, and the musician
seems to have been so thankful to find things no worse
that he took the young people's explanations in good part.
He would even seem to have made some sort of conditional promise that she should no longer be compelled
to perform in public after she had fulfilled existing engagements, and so brought her back peacefully to Bath.
Richard, who in the meantime, in his letters home, had
spoken of his bride as Miss L., announcing her settlement
in her convent, without the slightest intimation of any
claim on his part upon her, seems to have returned with
them; but no one, not even Miss Linley's father, was
informed of the Calais marriage, which seems, in all good
faith, to have been a form gone through in case any
scandal should be raised, but at present meaning nothing
more. And Bath, with all its scandal-mongers, at a
period when the general imagination was far from
delicate, seems to have accepted the escapade with a confidence in both the young people, and entire belief in their
honour, which makes us think better both of the age and
the town. We doubt whether such faith would be shown
in the hero and heroine of a similar freak in our own day.

Young Sheridan, however, came home to no peaceable reception. He had to meet his indignant brother in the first place, and to settle the question raised by the insulting advertisement of Matthews, which naturally set his youthful blood boiling. Before his return to Bath he had seen this villain in London, who had the audacity to disclaim the advertisement and attribute it to Charles Sheridan—a suggestion which naturally brought the young man home furious. The trembling sisters, delighted to welcome Richard, and, eager to know all about his adventure, had their natural sentiments checked by the gloomy looks with which the brothers met; and went to bed reluctantly that first evening, hearing the young men's voices high and angry, and anticipating with horror a quarrel between them. Next morning neither of them appeared. They had gone off again with those so-easily-obtained post-horses to London. A terrible time of waiting ensued; the distracted girls ran to the Linleys, but found no information there. They expected nothing better than to hear of a duel between their brothers for the too-charming Eliza's sake.

Hitherto, all has been the genteelest of comedy in fine eighteenth-century style : the villain intriguing, the ardent young lover stealing the lady out of his clutches, and Lydia Languish herself not without a certain delight in the romance, notwithstanding all her flutterings : the post-chaise dashing through the night, the alarms of the voyage, the curious innocent delusion of the marriage, complaisant priest and homely confidant, and guardian-bridegroom with a soul above every ungenerous advantage. But the following act is wildly sensational. The account of the brawl that follows is given at length by

all Sheridan's biographers. It is scarcely necessary to say
that when the brothers, angry as both were, had mutually
explained themselves, it was not to lift unnatural hands
against each other that they sallied forth, while the
girls lay listening and trembling upstairs, but to jump
once more into a post-chaise, and rattle over the long
levels of the Bath road to town through the dewy chill
of a May night, which did nothing, however, towards
cooling their hot blood. Before leaving Bath, Richard
had flashed forth a letter to the Master of the Ceremonies,
informing him that Matthews' conduct had been such
that no verbal apology could now be accepted from him.
The first step the hero took on arriving in London was
to challenge the villain, who indeed would seem to have
behaved as infamously as the most boldly-drawn villain
on the stage could be represented as doing. And then
comes a most curious scene. The gentlemen with their
rapiers go out to the Park, walking out together about
six in the evening, apparently a time when the Park was
almost empty ; but on various pretences the offender de-
clines to fight there, with an air of endeavouring to slip out
of the risk altogether. After several attempts to persuade
him to stand and draw, the party, growing more and more
excited, at length go to a coffee-house, "The Castle Tavern,
Henrietta Street"—having first called at two or three
other places, where their heated looks would seem to have
roused suspicion. Their march through the streets in the
summer evening on this strange errand, each with his
second, the very sword quivering at young Richard's side
and the blood boiling in his veins, among all the peaceful
groups streaming away from the Park, is wonderful
to think of. When they got admittance at last to a

private room in the tavern, the following scene occurs :—

"Mr. Ewart (the second of Sheridan) took lights up in his hand, and almost immediately on our entering the room we engaged. I struck Mr. Matthews' point so much out of the line that I stepped up and caught hold of his wrist, or the hilt of his sword, while the point of mine was at his breast. You (the letter is addressed to the second on the other side) ran in and caught hold of my arm, exclaiming— 'Don't kill him!' I struggled to disengage my arm, and said his sword was in my power. Mr. Matthews called out twice or thrice, 'I beg my life.' You immediately said 'There! he has begged his life, and now there is an end of it;' and on Mr. Ewart's saying that when his sword was in my power, as I attempted no more you should not have interfered, you replied that you were wrong, but that you had done it hastily and to prevent mischief—or words to that effect. Mr. Matthews then hinted that I was rather obliged to your interposition for the advantage : you declared that before you did so both the swords were in Mr. Sheridan's power. Mr. Matthews still seemed resolved to give it another turn, and observed that he had never quitted his sword. Provoked at this I then swore (with too much heat, perhaps) that he should either give up his sword and I would break it, or go to his guard again. He refused—but on my persisting either gave it into my hand, or flung it on the table or the ground (which, I will not absolutely affirm). I broke it and flung the hilt to the other end of the room. He exclaimed at this. I took a mourning sword from Mr. Ewart, and, presenting him with mine, gave my honour that what had passed should never be mentioned by me, and he might now right himself again. He replied that he 'would never draw a sword against the man that had given him his life'; but on his still exclaiming against the indignity of breaking his sword (which he had brought upon himself), Mr. Ewart offered him the pistols, and some altercation passed between them. Mr. Matthews said that he could never show his face if it were known that his sword was broke—that such a thing had never been done—that it cancelled all obligations, etc. You seemed

to think it was wrong, and we both proposed that if he never
misrepresented the affair it should not be mentioned by us.
This was settled. I then asked Mr. Matthews, as he had
expressed himself sensible of and shocked at the injustice and
indignity he had done me by his advertisement, whether it did
not occur to him that he owed me another satisfaction : and
that as it was now in his power to do it without discredit, I
supposed he would not hesitate. This he absolutely refused,
unless conditionally. I insisted on it, and said I would not
leave the room till it was settled. After much altercation,
and with much ill grace, he gave the apology."

There could not be a more curious scene. The out-
door duel is familiar enough both to fact and fiction;
but the flash of the crossing swords, the sudden rush, the
altercations of the angry group, the sullen submission of
the disarmed bully, going on by the light of the flaring
candles, in an inn-parlour, while the ordinary bustle of
the tavern proceeded peacefully below, is as strange a
picture as we can remember. Sheridan's account of the
circumstances was made in answer to another, which
stated them, as he asserts, falsely. The brothers returned home on Tuesday morning (they had left Bath
on Saturday night), "much fatigued, not having been
in bed since they left home," with Matthews' apology,
and triumph in their hearts, to the great consolation
and relief of the anxious girls. But their triumph
was not to be so easy. The circumstances of the duel
oozed out, as most things do, and Matthews, stung by
shame, challenged Sheridan again, choosing pistols as the
weapons, *prior to swords*, "from a conviction that Mr.
Sheridan would run in on him and an ungentlemanly
scuffle probably be the consequence." This presentiment
very evidently was justified; for the pistols were not
used, and the duel ended in a violent scuffle—not like

the usual dignified calm which characterises such deadly meetings. Matthews broke his sword upon Sheridan's ribs. The two antagonists fell together, Sheridan wounded and bleeding underneath, while the elder and heavier man punched at him with his broken sword. They were separated at length by the seconds, Sheridan refusing to "beg his life." He was carried home very seriously wounded, and, as was believed, in great danger. Miss Linley was singing at Oxford at the time, and while there Sheridan's wounded condition and the incident altogether was concealed from her, though everybody else knew of it and of her connection with it. When it was at last communicated to her, she almost betrayed their secret, which even now nobody suspected, by a cry of "My husband! my husband!" which startled all who were present, but was set down to her excitement and distress, and presently forgotten.

This tremendous encounter closed the episode. Matthews had vindicated his courage and obliterated the stigma of the broken sword, and though there was at one moment a chance of a third duel, thenceforward we hear little more of him. Sheridan recovered slowly under the care of his sisters, his father and brother being again absent and not very friendly. "We neither of us could approve of the cause in which you suffer," Charles writes. "All your friends here (in London) condemn you." The brother, however, has the grace to add that he is "unhappy at the situation I leave you in with respect to money matters," and that "Ewart was greatly vexed at the manner of your drawing for the last twenty pounds," so that it seems the respectable brandy-merchant had been the family stand-by. The poor young fellow's position was miser-

able enough—badly wounded, without a shilling, his love
sedulously kept away from him, and the bond between
them so strenuously ignored, that he promised his father,
with somewhat guilty disingenuousness, that he never
would marry Miss Linley.   Life was altogether at a low
ebb with him.   When he got better he was sent into the
country to Waltham Abbey, no doubt by way of weaning
him from all the seductions of Bath, and the vicinity of
the lovely young singer who had resumed her profession
though she hated it, and was to be seen of all men except
the faithful lover who was her husband, though nobody
knew.

Before we conclude this chapter of young life, which
reads so like an argument to the *Rivals* or some similar
play, we may indicate some of Sheridan's early productions which, common as the pretty art of verse-making
was, showed something more than the facile knack of
composition, which is one of what were entitled in
that day "the elegant qualifications" of golden youth.
Sacred to Eliza Linley, as well as the verses about
"the moss-covered grotto," was the following graceful
snatch of song, which is pretty enough to be got by
heart and sung by love-sick youths in many generations
to some pretty *rococo* air as fantastic as itself : —

> " Dry be that tear, my gentlest love,
>   Be hush'd that struggling sigh;
> Nor seasons, day, nor fate shall prove
>   More fix'd, more true than I.
> Hush'd be that sigh, be dry that tear,
> Cease boding doubt, cease anxious fear,
>   Dry be that tear.
>
> Ask'st thou how long my love will stay,
>   When all that's new is past?

How long, ah Delia, can I say,
  How long my life will last ?
Dry be that tear, be hush'd that sigh,
At least I'll love thee till I die.
      Hush'd be that sigh.

And does that thought affect thee too,
  The thought of Sylvio's death,
That he who only breath'd for you
Must yield his faithful breath?
Hush'd be that sigh, be dry that tear,
Nor let us lose our heaven here.
      Dry be that tear."

Moore, with a pedantry which is sufficiently absurd,
having just traced an expression in the "moss-covered
grotto" to a classical authority, though with a doubt very
favourable to his own scholarship, "whether Sheridan
was likely to have been a reader of Augurianus," finds a
close resemblance in the above to "one of the madrigals
of Montreuil," or perhaps to "an Italian song of Ménage."
Very likely it resembled all those pretty things, the
rococo age being not yet over and such elegant trifles
still in fashion—as indeed they will always be as long as
youth and its sweet follies last.

Other pretty bits of verse might be quoted, especially
one which brings in another delightful literary association
into the story. Lady Margaret Fordyce—the beloved sister
at whose departure from the old home in Fife Lady Anne
Lindsay was so dejected, that to console herself she sang
the woes, more plaintive still than her own, of that
immortal peasant lass who married Auld Robin Gray
—was then in Bath, and had been dismissed by a local
versifier in his description of the beauties of the place
by a couplet about a dimple, which roused young

Sheridan's wrath. "Could you," he cries, addressing the
poetaster—

> " Could you really discover,
>   In gazing those sweet beauties over,
>   No other charm, no winning grace,
>   Adorning either mind or face,
>   But one poor dimple to express
>   The quintessence of loveliness ?
>
>   Mark'd you her cheek of rosy hue ?
>   Mark'd you her eye of sparkling blue ?
>   That eye in liquid circles moving,
>   That cheek, abash'd at man's approving :
>   The one Love's arrows darting round,
>   The other blushing at the wound ;
>   Did she not speak, did she not move,
>   Now Pallas—now the Queen of Love ?"

The latter lines are often quoted, but it is pretty to
know that it was of Lady Anne's Margaret that they were
said.

It is probably also to his period of seclusion and
leisure at Waltham that the early dramatic attempts found
by Moore among the papers confided to him belong. One
of these runs to the length of three acts, and is a work of
the most fantastic description, embodying, so far as it
goes, the life of a band of outlaws calling themselves
Devils, who have their headquarters in a forest and keep
the neighbourhood in alarm. The heroine, a mysterious
and beautiful maiden, is secluded in a cave from which
she has never been allowed to go out, nor has she ever
seen the face of man except that of the old hermit, who
is her guardian. She has been permitted, however, one
glimpse of a certain young huntsman, whom she considers
a phantom, until a second sight of him when he is taken

prisoner by the robbers, and unaccountably introduced into
the cave where she lies asleep, convinces her of his reality,
and naturally has the same effect upon her which the
sudden apparition of Prince Ferdinand had upon Miranda.
The scene is pretty enough as the work of a sentimental
youth in an age addicted to the highflown everywhere,
and especially on the stage.   The hero, when unbound
and left to himself, begins his soliloquy, as a matter of
course, with a "Ha! where am I?" but changes his tone
from despair to rapture when he sees the fair Reginilla
whose acquaintance he had so mysteriously made.   "Oh,
would she but wake and bless this gloom with her bright
eyes," he says, after half a page.   "Soft, here's a lute :
perhaps her soul will know the call of harmony."   Mrs.
Radcliffe's lovely heroines, at a still later period, carried
their lutes about with them everywhere, and tuned them
to the utterance of a favourite copy of verses in the most
terrible circumstances ; so that the discovery of so handy
an instrument in a robber's cave occasioned no surprise
to the young hero.   The song he immediately sung has
been, Moore confesses, manipulated by himself.   "I have
taken the liberty of supplying a few rhymes and words
that are wanting," he says, so that we need not quote it
as an example of Sheridan.   But the performance has its
desired effect and the lady wakes.

" *Reg.* (*waking*). The phantom, father ! (*seizes his hand*)
Oh, do not—do not wake me thus.
Huntsman (*kneeling*). Thou beauteous sun of this dark
world, that mak'st a place so like the cave of death a heaven
to me, instruct me how I may approach thee—how address
thee and not offend.
Reg. Oh, how my soul could hang upon those lips.   Speak

on ! and yet methinks he should not kneel. Why are you afraid, sir ? indeed I cannot hurt you.

Hunts. Sweet Innocence, I am sure thou would'st not.

Reg. Art thou not he to whom I told my name, and did'st thou not say thine was ——

Hunts. Oh blessed was the name that then thou told'st— it has been ever since my charm and kept me from distraction. But may I ask how such sweet excellence as thine could be hid in such a place ?

Reg. Alas ! I know not—for such as thou I never saw before, nor any like myself.

Hunts. Nor like thee ever shall ; but would'st leave this place and live with such as I am ?

Reg. Why may not you live here with such as I ?

Hunts. Yes, but I would carry thee where all above an azure canopy extends, at night bedropt with gems, and one more glorious lamp that yields such beautiful light as love enjoys ; while underneath a carpet shall be spread of flowers to court the presence of thy step, with such sweet-whispered invitations from the leaves of shady groves or murmuring of silver streams, that thou shalt think thou art in paradise.

Reg. Indeed !

Hunts. Ay, and I'll watch and wait on thee all day, and cull the choicest flowers, which while thou bind'st in the mysterious knot of love, I'll tune for thee no vulgar lays, or tell thee tales shall make thee weep, yet please thee, while thus I press thy hand, and warm it thus with kisses.

Reg. I doubt thee not—but then my Governor has told me many a tale of faithless men, who court a lady but to steal her peace. . . . Then, wherefore could'st thou not live here ? For I do feel, though tenfold darkness did surround this spot, I would be blest would you but stay here ; and if it make you sad to be imprisoned thus, I'd sing and play for thee, and dress thee sweetest fruits, and though you chide me would kiss thy tears away, and hide my blushing face upon thy bosom : indeed I would. Then what avails the gaudy days, and all the evil things I'm told inhabit them, to those who have within themselves all that delight and love and heaven can give ?

Hunts. My angel, thou hast indeed the soul of love.

Reg. It is no ill thing, is it ?

Hunts. Oh most divine—it is the immediate gift of heaven ——"

And then the lute is brought into requisition once more. Other scenes of a much less superfine description, in one of which the hero takes the semblance of a dancing bear, go on outside this sentimental retirement, and some humour is expended on the trial of various prisoners secured by the robbers, who are made to believe that they have left this world and are being brought up before a kind of Pluto for judgment. This inflexible judge orders "baths of flaming sulphur and the caldron of boiling lead" for one who confesses himself to have been a courtier; the culprit's part, however, is taken by a compassionate devil who begs that he may be soaked a little first in scalding brimstone to prepare him for his final sentence.

Another unfinished sketch called the *Foresters* deals with effects not quite so violent. To the end of his life Sheridan would threaten smilingly to produce this play and outdo everything else with it, but the existing framework seems to have been of the very slightest. Probably to a much later period belongs the projected play upon the subject of *Affectation*, for which were intended many memorandums found written upon the paper books in which his thoughts were noted. The subject is one which, in the opinion of various critics, would have been specially adapted to Sheridan's powers, and Moore, and many others following him, express regret that it should have been abandoned. But no doubt Sheridan's instinct warned him that on no such set plan could his faculties work, and that the stage, however adapted to the display of individual eccen-

tricities, wants something more than a bundle of em-
bodied *fads* to make its performances tell. Sir Bubble
Bon, Sir Peregrine Paradox, the representative "man who
delights in hurry and interruption," the "man intriguing
only for the reputation of it," the "lady who affects
poetry," and all the rest, do well enough for the table-
talk of the imagination, or even to jot down and play with
in a note-book; but Sheridan was better inspired than to
attempt to make them into a play. He had already
among these memorandums of his the first ideas of almost
all his future productions, the primitive notes afterwards
to be developed into the brilliant malice of the scandal-
mongers, the first conception of old Teazle, the earliest
adumbration of the immortal Puff. But the little verses
which we have already quoted were the best of his actual
achievements at this early period, dictated as they were
by the early passion which made the careless boy into
a man.

At least one other poetical address of a similar description—stilted, yet not without a tender breath of
pastoral sweetness—was addressed to Eliza after she
became Sheridan's wife, and told how Silvio reclined
upon "Avon's ridgy bank"—

> "Did mock the meadow's flowing pride,
>   Rail'd at the dawn and sportive ring;
> The tabour's call he did deride
>   And said, It was not Spring.
>
> He scorned the sky of azure blue,
>   He scorned whate'er could mirth bespeak,
> He chid the beam that drank the dew,
>   And chid the gale that fanned his glowing cheek.
> Unpaid the season's wonted lay,
> For still he sighed and said, It was not May."

Which is of course explained by the circumstance that Delia (for the nonce called Laura) was not there. Laura responded in verses not much worse. It was a pretty commerce, breathing full of the time when shepherds and shepherdesses were still the favourites of dainty poetry—a fashion which seems in some danger of returning with the other quaintnesses of the time. But this was after the young pair were united; and in 1772, when he had recovered of his wounds, and was making what shift he could to occupy himself in the solitude of Waltham, studying a little for a variety, reading up the History of England and the works of Sir William Temple, by way of improving his mind, that blessed event seemed distant and unlikely enough.

In the Lent of 1773, Miss Linley came to London to sing in the oratorios, and it is said that young Sheridan resorted to the most romantic expedients to see her. He was near enough to "tread on the heels of perilous probabilities,"—a phrase which Moore quotes from one of his letters,—and is said to have come from Waltham to London, and to have disguised himself as a hackney coachman, and driven her home from her performances on several occasions. The anonymous author of *Sheridan and his Times* asserts that on one of these occasions, by some accident, the lady was alone, and that this opportunity of communication led to a series of meetings, which at length convinced the parents that further resistance was hopeless. During all this time it would appear the marriage at Calais was never referred to, and was thought nothing of, even by the parties most concerned. It was intended apparently as a safeguard to Delia's reputation should need occur, but as nothing

more; which says a great deal for the romantic generosity of so ardent a lover and so penniless a man. For
Delia had her little fortune, besides all the other charms
which spoke so much more eloquently to her Silvio's
heart, and was indeed a liberal income in herself, to any
one who would take advantage of it, with that lovely
voice of hers. But the young man was romantically
magnanimous and highflying in his sense of honour.
He was indeed a very poor match,—a youth without a
penny, even without a profession, and no visible means
of living,—for the adored siren, about whom wealthy
suitors were dangling by the dozen, no doubt exciting
many anxious hopes in the breasts of her parents, if
not in her own faithful bosom. But love conquered in
the long run, as an honest and honourable sentiment,
if it lasts and can wait, is pretty sure to do. In April
1773, about a year from the time of their clandestine
marriage at Calais, they were married in the eye of day,
with all that was needful to make the union dignified
and respectable; and thus the bustling little romance so
full of incident, so entirely ready for the use of the
drama, so like all the favourite stage-combinations of the
time, came to an end. We do not hear very much of
Mrs. Sheridan afterwards: indeed, except the letter to
which we have referred, she does little to disclose her
personality at any time, but there is something engaging
and attractive—a sort of faint but sweet reflection raying
out from her through all her life. The Lydia Languish
of early days—the sentimental and romantic heroine of
so many persecutions and pursuits, of the midnight flight
and secret marriage—developed into one of those favourites of society, half-artist, half-fine-lady, whose exertions

for the amusement of the world bring nothing to them
but a half-fictitious position and dangerous flatteries,
without even the public singer's substantial reward—a
class embracing many charming and attractive women,
victims of their own gifts and graces. Mrs. Sheridan
was, however, at the same time—at least in all the early
part of her career—a devoted wife, and seems to have
done her best for her brilliant husband, and formed
no small item in his success as well as in his happiness
as long as her existence lasted. It is said that she
disliked the life of a singer, and it is certain that she
acquiesced in his resolution to withdraw her from all
public appearances; but even in that point it is very
likely that there was some unconsidered sacrifice in
her submission. "Hers was truly a voice as of the
church choir," says a contemporary quoted by Moore,
"and she was always ready to sing without any pressing.
She sang here a great deal and to my infinite delight:
but what had a peculiar charm was that she used to
take my daughter, then a child, on her lap, and sing a
number of childish songs with such a playfulness of
manner and such a sweetness of look and voice as was
quite enchanting."

CHAPTER II.

MARRIED at last and happy, after so much experience of
disappointment and hope deferred, Sheridan and his
young wife took a cottage in the country, and retired
there to enjoy their long-wished-for life together, and to
consider an important, but it would seem not absolutely
essential point—what they were to do for their living.
Up to this point they have been so entirely the personages of a drama, that it is quite in order that they
should retire to a rose-covered cottage, with nothing particular to live upon; and that the young husband, though
without any trade of his own by which he could earn a
dinner, should magnificently waive off all offers of employment for his wife, who had a trade—and a profitable one.
He was still but twenty-two and she nineteen, and he
had hitherto managed to get all that was necessary, besides post-chaises and a considerable share of the luxuries
of the time, as the lilies get their bravery, without toil-
ing or spinning, so that it is evident the young man confronted fate with very little alarm, and his proud attitude
of family head and master of his own wife is in the highest degree edifying as well as amusing. We can scarcely

help doubting greatly whether a prima donna even of
nineteen would let herself be disposed of now by such
an absolute authority. The tone of the letter in which
he communicates to his father-in-law his lofty determination in this respect will show the young men of to-day
the value of the privileges which they have, it is to be
feared, partially resigned.

"Yours of the 3d instant did not reach me till yesterday,
by reason of its missing us at Morden. As to the principal
point it treats of, I had given my answer some days ago to
Mr. Isaac of Worcester. He had enclosed a letter from
Storace to my wife, in which he dwells much on the nature of
the agreement you had made for her eight months ago, and
adds that ' as this is no new application, but a request that
you (Mrs. S.) will fulfil a positive engagement, the breach of
which would prove of fatal consequence to our meeting, I
hope Mr. Sheridan will think his honour in some degree concerned in fulfilling it.' Mr. Storace, in order to enforce Mr.
Isaac's argument, showed me his letter on the same subject to
him, which begins with saying, ' We must have Mrs. Sheridan
somehow or other if possible, the plain English of which is
that if her husband is not willing to let her perform, we will
persuade him that he acts *dishonourably* in preventing her
from fulfilling a positive engagement.' This I conceive to
be the very worst mode of application that could have been
taken ; as there really is not common sense in the idea that
my *honour* can be concerned in my wife's fulfilling an engagement which it is impossible she should ever have made.
Nor (as I wrote to Mr. Isaac) can you who gave the promise,
whatever it was, be in the least charged with the breach of it,
as your daughter's marriage was an event which must always
have been looked to by them as quite as natural a period to
your rights over her as her death. And in my opinion it
would have been just as reasonable to have applied to you to
fulfil your engagement in the latter case than in the former.
As to the imprudence of declining this engagement, I do not
think, even were we to suppose that my wife should ever on

any occasion appear again in public, there would be the least at present. For instance, I have had a gentleman with me from Oxford (where they do not claim the least right as from an engagement) who has endeavoured to place the idea of my complimenting the university with Betsey's performance in the strongest light of advantage to me. This he said on my declining to let her perform on any agreement. He likewise informed me that he had just left Lord North (the Chancellor), who, he assured me, would look upon it as the highest compliment, and had expressed himself so to him. Now, should it be a point of inclination or convenience to me to break my resolution with regard to Betsey's performing, there surely would be more sense in obliging Lord North (and probably from his own application) than Lord Coventry and Mr. Isaac ; for were she to sing at Worcester, there would not be the least compliment in her performing at Oxford."

The poor pretty wife, smiling passive in the background while my young lord considers whether he will "compliment the university" with her performance, is a spectacle which ought to be impressive to the brides of the present day, who take another view of their position ; but there is a delightful humour in this turning of the tables upon the stern father who had so often snubbed young Sheridan, and who must have regarded, one would suppose, his present impotence and the sublime superiority of the new proprietor of Betsey with anything but pleasant feelings. Altogether the attitude of the group is very instructive in view of the changes of public opinion on this point. The most arbitrary husband now-a-days would think it expedient at least to associate his wife's name with his own in any such refusal ; but the proprietorship was undoubting in Sheridan's day. It will be remembered that Dr. Johnson highly applauded the young gentleman's spirit and resolution in this point.

However, though she had so soon become Betsey and his property, so far as business was concerned, the cottage at East Burnham among the beech trees and roses, still contained a tender pair of lovers; and Silvio still addressed to Delia the sweetest compliments in verse. When he is absent he appeals to Hymen to find some thing for him to do to make the hours pass when away from her.

> " Alas ! thou hast no wings, oh Time,
> It was some thoughtless lover's rhyme,
> Who, writing in his Chloe's view,
> Paid her the compliment through you.
> For had he, if he truly lov'd,
> But once the pangs of absence prov'd,
> He'd cropt thy wings, and in their stead
> Have painted thee with heels of lead."

Thus Betsey's chains were gilded: and in all likelihood she was totally unconscious of them, never having been awakened to any right of womankind beyond that of being loved and flattered. The verse is not of very high quality, but the sentiment is charming, and entirely appropriate to the position.

> " For me who, when I'm happy, owe
> No thanks to fortune that I'm so,
> Who long have learn'd to look at one
> Dear object, and at one alone,
> For all the joy and all the sorrow,
> That gilds the day or threats the morrow.
> I never felt thy footsteps light
> But when sweet love did aid thy flight,
> And banished from his blest dominion,
> I car'd not for thy borrowed pinion.
>   True, she is mine ; and since she's mine
>   At trifles I should not repine ;
>   But oh ! the miser's real pleasure
>   Is not in knowing he has treasure ;

He must behold his golden store,
And feel and count his riches o'er.
Thus I of one dear gem possest,
And in that treasure only blest,
There every day would seek delight,
And clasp the casket every night."

The condition of the young pair in any reasonable
point of view at this beginning of their life was as little
hopeful as can be conceived. The three thousand pounds
left to Miss Linley by Mr. Long was their sole fortune, if
it still remained intact. The wife was rendered helpless by the husband's grand prohibition of her exertions,
and he himself had nothing to do, nor knew how to do
anything : for even to literature, that invariable refuge,
he scarcely seems as yet to have turned his eyes with any
serious intent. The manner in which they plunged into
life, however, is characteristic. When winter made their
Burnham cottage undesirable, and the time of honey-
mooning was well over, they went to town to live with
the composer Storace, where no doubt Betsey's talent was
largely exercised, though not in public, and probably
helped to make friends for the young pair : for we hear
of them next year as paying visits among other places
at the house of Canning ; and in the winter of 1774
they established themselves in Orchard Street, Portman
Square, in a house of their own, furnished, an anonymous biographer says, "in the most costly style," at the
expense of Linley, with perhaps some contribution
from that inexhaustible three thousand pounds.

"His house was open," says this historian, "for the reception of guests of quality attracted by his wit, the superior
accomplishments of his wife, and the elegance of his enter-

E

tainments.   His dinners were upon the most expensive scale,
his wines of the finest quality : while Mrs. Sheridan's soirées
were remarkable not more for their brilliance than the gay
groups of the most beautiful, accomplished, and titled lady
visitants of the Court of St. James.   Mrs. Sheridan's routs
were the great attraction of the season.   A friend—a warm
and sincere friend—remonstrating with Sheridan on the in-
stability of his means of supporting such a costly establishment, he tersely replied, ' My dear friend, it is my means.' "

Such a description will be taken for what it is worth,
but there seems internal evidence that the anecdote with
which it concludes might have been true.   And certainly
for a young man beginning the arduous occupation of
living on his wits, a pretty house and prettier wife and
good music would form an excellent stock-in-trade, and
the new home itself being entirely beyond any visible
means they had, every other prodigality would be comprehensible.   By this time he had begun the composition
of a play, and considered himself on the eve of publish-
ing a book, which, he " thinks, will do me some credit,"
as he informs his father-in-law, but which has never
been heard of from that time to this, so far as appears.
Another piece of information contained in the letter in
which this apocryphal work is announced, shows for the
first time a better prospect for the young adventurer.
He adds, " There will be a comedy of mine in rehearsal
at Covent Garden within a few days."

" I have done it at Mr. Harris's (the manager's) own request :
it is now complete in his hands, and preparing for the stage.
He and some of his friends also who have heard it assure me
in the most flattering terms that there is not a doubt of its success.   It will be very well played, and Harris tells me that the
least shilling I shall get (if it succeeds) will be six hundred
pounds.   I shall make no secret of it towards the time of

representation, that it may not lose any support my friends
can give it.   I had not written a line of it two months ago,
except a scene or two, which I believe you have seen in an
odd act of a little farce."

This was the *Rivals*, which was performed at Covent
Garden on the 17th January 1775—nearly three years
after his marriage.   How he existed in the meantime,
and made friends and kept up his London house, is left
to the imagination.   Probably it was done upon that
famous three thousand pounds, which appears, like the
widow's cruse, to answer all demands.

The *Rivals* was not successful the first night, and the
hopes of the young dramatist must have met with a
terrible check; but the substitution of one actor for
another in the part of Sir Lucius O'Trigger, and such
emendations as practical sense suggested as soon as it
had been put on the stage, secured for it one continued
triumph ever after.   It is now more than a century
since critical London watched the new comedy, and the
hearts of the Linleys thrilled from London to Bath, and
old Thomas Sheridan, still unreconciled to his son, came
silent and sarcastic to the theatre to see what the young
good-for-nothing had made of it; but the world has
never changed its opinion.   What a moment for Betsey
in the house where she had everything that heart of
woman could desire except the knowledge that all was
honest and paid for—a luxury which outdoes all the rest!
and for her husband, standing in the wings watching his
father's face, whom he dared not go and speak to, and
knowing that his whole future hung in the balance, and
that in case of success all his follies would be justified!
"But now there can be no doubt of its success," cries

little Miss Linley from Bath, in a flutter of excitement,
"as it has certainly got through more difficulties than
any comedy which has not met its doom the first night."
The Linleys were convinced in their own minds that it
was Mrs. Sheridan who had written "the much admired
epilogue." "How I long to read it!" cries the little
sister. "What makes it more certain is that my *father*
guessed it was *yours* the first time he saw it praised in
the paper." There is no reason to suppose that the guess
was true, but it is a pretty exhibition of family feeling.

The *Rivals*, to the ordinary spectator who, looking on
with uncritical pleasure at the progress of that episode of
mimic life, in which everybody's remarks are full of such
a quintessence of wit as only a very few remarkable persons are able to emulate in actual existence, accepts the
piece for the sake of these and other qualities—is so little
like a transcript from any actual conditions of humanity
that to consider it as studied from the life would be
absurd, and we receive these creations of fancy as belonging to a world entirely apart from the real. But the
reader who has accompanied Sheridan through the
previous chapter of his history will be inclined, on
the contrary, to feel that the young dramatist has
but selected a few incidents from the still more curious
comedy of life in which he himself had so recently
been one of the actors, and in which elopements,
duels, secret correspondences, and all the rest of the
simple-artificial round, were the order of the day.
Whether he drew his characters from the life it is needless to inquire, or if there was an actual prototype for Mrs.
Malaprop. Nothing, however, in imagination is so highly
fantastical as reality ; and it is very likely that some two

or three ladies of much pretension and gentility flourished upon the parade and frequented the pump-room, from whose conversation her immortal parts of speech were appropriated : but this is of very little importance in comparison with the delightful success of the result. The *Rivals* is no such picture of life in Bath as that which, half a century later, in altered times, which yet were full of humours of their own, Miss Austen made for us in all the modest flutter of youthful life and hopes.   Sheridan's brilliant dramatic sketch is slight in comparison, though far more instantly effective, and with a concentration in its sharp effects which the stage requires.   But yet, no doubt, in the bustle and hurry of the successive arrivals, in the eager brushing up of the countryman new-launched on such a scene, and the aspect of the idle yet bustling society, all agog for excitement and pleasure, the brisk little holiday city was delightfully recognisable in the eyes of those to whom "the Bath" represented all those vacation rambles and excursions over the world which amuse our leisure now.   Scarcely ever was play so full of liveliness and interest constructed upon a slighter machinery.   The Rivals of the title, by means of the most simple yet amusing of mystifications, are one person.   The gallant young lover, who is little more than the conventional type of that well-worn character, but a manly and lively one, has introduced himself to the romantic heroine in the character of Ensign Beverley, a poor young subaltern, instead of his own much more eligible personality as the heir of Sir Anthony Absolute, a baronet with four thousand a year : and has gained the heart of the sentimental Lydia, who prefers love in a cottage to the finest settlements, and looks forward to an elopement and the loss of a great part of her fortune with delight : when his plans are suddenly confounded by the arrival of his father on the scene, bent on marrying him forthwith in his own character to the same lady.   Thus he is at the same time the romantic and adored Beverley, and the detested Captain Absolute in her eyes ; and how to reconcile her to marrying peaceably and with the approval of all her belongings, instead of clandestinely and with all the *éclat* of a secret running away, is the problem.   This, however, is solved precipitately by the expedient of a duel with the third rival, Bob Acres, which shows the fair Lydia that the safety of her Beverley, even if accompanied by the congratulations of friends and a humdrum marriage, is the one thing to be desired.   Thus the whole action of the piece turns upon a mystification, which affords some delightfully comic scenes, but few of those occasions of suspense and uncertainty which give interest to the drama.   This we find in the brisk and delightful movement of the piece, in the broad but most amusing sketches of character, and the unfailing wit and sparkle of the dialogue.   In fact we believe that many an audience has enjoyed the play, and, what is more wonderful, many a reader laughed over it in private, without any clear realisation of the story at all, so completely do Sir Anthony's fits of temper, and Mrs. Malaprop's fine language and stately presence, and the swagger of Bob Acres, occupy and amuse us.   Even Faulkland, the jealous and doubting, who invents a new misery for himself at every word, and finds an occasion for wretchedness even in the smiles of his mistress, which are always either too cold or too warm for him, is so laughable in his starts aside at every new suggestion of jealous fancy, that we forgive him not only a great deal of fine language, but the still greater drawback of having nothing to do with the action of the piece at all.

Mrs. Malaprop's ingenious "derangement of epitaphs" is her chief distinction to the popular critic; and even though such a great competitor as Dogberry has occupied the ground before her, these delightful absurdities have never been surpassed. But justice has hardly been done to the individual character of this admirable if broad sketch of a personage quite familiar in such scenes as that which Bath presented a century ago, the plausible well-bred woman, with a great deal of vanity, and no small share of good-nature, whose inversion of phrases is quite representative of the blurred realisation she has of surrounding circumstances, and who is quite sincerely puzzled by the discovery that she is not so well qualified to enact the character of Delia as her niece would be. Mrs. Malaprop has none of the harshness of Mrs. Hardcastle in *She Stoops to Conquer*, and we take it unkind of Captain Absolute to call her "a weatherbeaten she-dragon." The complacent nod of her head, the smirk on her face, her delightful self-satisfaction and confidence in her "parts of speech," have nothing repulsive in them. No doubt she imposed upon Bob Acres; and could Catherine Morland and Mrs. Allen have seen her face and heard her talk, these ladies would, we feel sure, have been awed by her presence. And she is not unkind to Lydia, though the minx deserves it, and has no desire to appropriate her fortune. She smiles upon us still in many a watering-place—large, gracious, proud of her conversational powers, always a delightful figure to meet with, and filling the shopkeeping ladies with admiration.

Sir Anthony, though so amusing on the stage, is more
conventional, since we know he must get angry presently
whenever we meet with him, although his coming round
again is equally certain : but Mrs. Malaprop is never
quite to be calculated upon, and is always capable of
a new simile as captivating as that of the immortal
"allegory on the banks of the Nile."

The other characters, though full of brilliant talk,
cleverness, and folly, have less originality.   The country
hobbledehoy, matured into a dandy and braggart by
his entrance into the intoxicating excitement of Bath
society, is comical in the highest degree ; but he is not
characteristically human.   While Mrs. Malaprop can
hold her ground with Dogberry, Bob Acres is not fit to
be mentioned in the same breath with the "exquisite
reasons" of that delightful knight, Sir Andrew Ague-
cheek.   And thus it becomes at once apparent that
Sheridan's eye for a situation, and the details that
make up a striking combination on the stage, was far
more remarkable than his insight into human motives
and action.   There is no scene on the stage which re-
tains its power of amusing an ordinary audience more
brilliantly than that of the proposed duel, where the
wittiest of boobies confesses to feeling his valour ooze
out at his finger ends, and the fire-eating Sir Lucius
promises, to console him, that he shall be pickled and
sent home to rest with his fathers, if not content with
the snug lying in the abbey.   The two men are little
more than symbols of the slightest description, but their
dialogue is instinct with wit, and that fun, the most
English of qualities, which does not reach the height of
humour, yet overwhelms even gravity itself with a

laughter in which there is no sting or bitterness. Molière sometimes attains this effect, but rarely, having too much meaning in him ; but with Shakespeare it is frequent among higher things. And in Sheridan this gift of innocent ridicule and quick embodiment of the ludicrous without malice or *arrière-pensée* reaches to such heights of excellence as have given his nonsense a sort of immortality.

It is, however, difficult to go far in discussion or analysis of a literary production which attempts no deeper investigation into human nature than this. Sheridan's art, from its very beginning, was theatrical, if we may use the word, rather than dramatic. It aimed at strong situations and highly effective scenes rather than at a finely constructed story, or the working out of either plot or passion. There is nothing to be discovered in it by the student, as in those loftier dramas which deal with the higher qualities and developments of the human spirit. It is possible to excite a very warm controversy in almost any company of ordinarily educated people at any moment upon the character of Hamlet. And criticism will always find another word to say even upon the less profound but delightful mysteries of such a poetical creation as Rosalind, all glowing with ever-varied life and love and fancy. But the lighter drama with which we have now to deal hides no depths under its brilliant surface. The pretty fantastical Lydia, with her romances, her impatience of ordinary life, her hot little spark of temper, was new to the stage, and when she finds a fitting representative can be made delightful upon it : but there is nothing further to find out about her. The art is charming, the figures full of vivacity,

the touch that sets them before us exquisite : except
indeed in the Faulkland scenes, probably intended as a
foil for the brilliancy of the others, in which Julia's magnificent phrases are too much for us, and make us deeply
grateful to Sheridan for the discrimination which kept
him — save in one appalling instance—from the serious
drama. But there are no depths to be sounded, and no
suggestions to be carried out. While, however, its merits
as literature are thus lessened, its attractions as a play are
increased. There never was a comedy more dear to actors,
as there never was one more popular on the stage. The
even balance of its characters, the equality of the parts,
scarcely one of them being quite insignificant, and each
affording scope enough for a good player to show what is
in him, must make it always popular in the profession.
It is, from the same reason, the delight of amateurs.

Moore quotes from an old copy of the play, a humorous dedication written by Tickell, Sheridan's brother-in-
law, to Indolence. "There is a propriety in prefixing
your name to a work begun entirely at your suggestion
and finished under your auspices," Tickell says; and
notwithstanding his biographer's attempt to prove that
Sheridan polished all he wrote with extreme care, and
cast and recast his literary efforts, there is an air of ease
and lightness in his earlier work which makes the dedication sufficiently appropriate. It must have amused his
own fancy while he wrote, as it has amused his audience
ever since. It is the one blossom of production which
had yet appeared in so many easy years. A wide margin
of leisure, of pleasure, of facile life, extends around it.
It was done quickly it appears when once undertaken—a
pleasing variety upon the featureless course of months

and years. The preface which Sheridan himself prefixed to the play when printed, justifies itself on the score that "the success of the piece has probably been founded on a circumstance which the author is informed has not before attended a theatrical trial."

"I need scarcely add that the circumstance alluded to was the withdrawing of the piece to remove these imperfections in the first representation which were too obvious to escape reprehension, and too numerous to admit of a hasty correction. . . . It were unnecessary to enter into any further extenuation of what was thought exceptionable in this play, but that it has been said that the managers should have prevented some of the defects before its appearance to the public—and, in particular, the uncommon length of the piece as represented the first night. It were an ill return for the most liberal and gentlemanly conduct on their side to suffer any censure to rest where none was deserved. Hurry in writing has long been exploded as an excuse for an author ; however, in the dramatic line, it may happen that both an author and a manager may wish to fill a chasm in the entertainment of the public with a hastiness not altogether culpable. The season was advanced when I first put the play into Mr. Harris's hands ; it was at that time at least double the length of any acting comedy. I profited by his judgment and experience in the curtailing of it, till I believe his feeling for the vanity of a young author got the better of his desire for correctness, and he left so many excrescences remaining because he had assisted in pruning so many more. Hence, though I was not uninformed that the acts were still too long, I flattered myself that after the first trial I might with safer judgment proceed to remove what should appear to have been most dissatisfactory."

These were, it is true, days of leisure, when nothing was pushed and hurried on as now. But it would require, one would think, no little firmness and courage on the part of a young author to risk the emendation of errors so serious after an unfavourable first-night, and a great

confidence on the part of the manager to permit such
an experiment. But there are some men who impress
all around them with such a certainty of power and
success, that even managers dare, and publishers volun-
teer, in their favour. Sheridan was evidently one of
these men. There was an atmosphere of triumph about
him. He had carried off his siren from all competitors; he had defied all inducements to give her up to
public hearing after; he had flown in the face of prudence and every frugal tradition. And so far as an easy
and happy life went, he was apparently succeeding in
that attempt. So he was allowed to take his unsuc-
cessful comedy off the stage, and trim it into his own
guise of triumph. We are not told how long the interval
was, which would have been instructive (the anonymous
biographer says "a few days"). It was produced in
January, however, and a month later we hear of it in preparation at Bath, where its success was extraordinary.
The same witness, whom we have just quoted, adds, "that
Sheridan's prospective six hundred pounds was more than
doubled by its success and the liberality of the manager."

He had thus entered fully upon his career as a dramatist. In the same year he wrote—in gratitude, it is
said, to the Irish actor who had saved the *Rivals* by his
felicitous representation of Sir Lucius—the farce called *St.
Patrick's Day ; or, the Scheming Lieutenant*, a very slight
production, founded on the tricks so familiar to comedy,
of a lover's ingenuity to get entrance into the house of
his mistress. The few opening sentences, which are
entirely characteristic of Sheridan, are almost the best
part of the production : they are spoken by a party of
soldiers coming with a complaint to their officer.

"*1st Sol.* I say, you are wrong ; we should all speak together, each for himself, and all at once, that we may be
heard the better.

2d Sol. Right, Jack ; we'll argue in platoons.

3d Sol. Ay, ay, let him have our grievances in a volley."

The lieutenant, whose suit is scorned by the parents
of his Lauretta, contrives by the aid of a certain Dr.
Rosy, a comic, but not very comic, somewhat long-winded
personage, to get into the house of Justice Credulous,
her father, as a servant : but is discovered and turned
out. He then writes a letter asserting that, in his
first disguise, he has given the Justice poison, an assertion which is met with perfect faith ; upon which
he comes in again as the famous quack doctor, so
familiar to us in the pages of Molière. In this case
the quack is a German, speaking only a barbarous
jargon, but he speedily cures the Justice on condition of
receiving the hand of his daughter. "Did he say all that
in so few words," cried Justice Credulous, when one of
the stranger's utterances is explained to him. "What a
fine language it is !"—just as M. Jourdain delightedly
acknowledged the eloquence of *la langue Turque*, which
could express *tant de choses dans un seul mot.* The *Scheming
Lieutenant* still keeps its ground among Sheridan's works,
bound up between the *Rivals* and the *School for Scandal*,
a position in which one cannot help feeling it must be
much astonished to find itself.

In the end of the year the opera of the *Duenna* was
also produced at Covent Garden. The praise and immediate appreciation with which it was received were still
greater than those that hailed the *Rivals.* "The run of
this opera has, I believe, no parallel in the annals of the

drama," says Moore, speaking in days when the theatre
had other rules than those known among ourselves.
"Sixty-three nights was the career of the *Beggar's Opera ;*
but the *Duenna* was acted no less than seventy-five times
during the season," and the enthusiasm which it called forth
was general. It was pronounced better than the *Beggar's
Opera*, up to that time acknowledged to be the first and
finest production of the never very successful school of
English opera. Opera at all was as yet an exotic in England, and the public still resented the importation of Italian
music and Italian singers to give it utterance, and fondly
clung to the idea of being able to produce as good or better
at home. The *Duenna* was a joint work in which Sheridan
was glad to associate with himself his father-in-law, Linley, whose airs to the songs, which were plentifully introduced—and which gave its name to what is in reality a
short comedy on the lines of Molière, interspersed with
songs, and not an opera in the usual sense of the word
at all—were much commended at the time. The little
lyrics which are put indiscriminately into the mouths of
the different personages are often extremely pretty ; but
few people in these days have heard them sung, though
lines from the verses are still familiar enough to our ears
in the way of quotation. The story of the piece belongs
to the same easy artificial inspiration which dictated the
trivial plot of *St. Patrick's Day*, and of so many others. It
is "mainly founded," says Moore, "upon an incident borrowed from the *Country Wife* of Wycherley," but it seems
hardly necessary to seek a parent for so *banal* a contrivance. The father, with whom we are all so familiar, has
to be tricked out of his daughter by one of the mono-
tonous lovers with whom we are more familiar still ; but

instead of waiting till her gallant shall invent a plan for
this purpose, the lady cuts the knot herself by the help
of her duenna, who has no objection to marry the rich
Jew whom Louisa abhors, and who remains in the garb
of her young mistress, while the latter escapes in the
duenna's hood and veil. The Portuguese Isaac from
whom the lady flies is a crafty simpleton, and when he
finds the old duenna waiting for him under the name of
Louisa (whom her father, for the convenience of the plot,
has vowed never to see till she is married), he accepts her,
though much startled by her venerable and unlovely appearance, as the beautiful creature who has been promised
to him, with only the rueful reflection to himself, "How
blind some parents are!" and as she explains that she
also has made a vow never to accept a husband from her
father's hands, carries her off, as she suggests, with much
simplicity and the astute reflection, "If I take her at her
word I secure her fortune and avoid making any settlement in return." In the meantime two pairs of interesting lovers, Louisa and her Antonio, her brother Ferdinand and his Clara, are wandering about in various
disguises, with a few quarrels and reconciliations, and a
great many songs, which they pause to sing at the most
inappropriate moments, after the fashion of opera. In
order to be married—which all are anxious to be—Isaac
and one of the young gallants go to a "neighbouring
monastery," such establishments being delightfully handy
in Seville, where the scene is laid; and the hot Protest-
antism of the audience is delighted by an ecclesiastical
interior, in which "Father Paul, Father Francis, and
other friars are discovered at a table drinking," singing
convivial songs, and promising to remember their peni-

tents in their cups, which will do quite as much good as masses. Father Paul is the supposed ascetic of the party, and comes forward when called with a glass of wine in his hand, chiding them for having disturbed his devotions. The three couples are then married by this worthy functionary, and the whole ends with a scene at the house of the father, when the trick is revealed to him, and amid general blessings and forgiveness the Jew discovers that he has married the penniless duenna instead of the lady with a fortune, whom he has helped to deceive himself as well as her father. The duenna, who has been, like all the old ladies in these plays, the subject of a great many unmannerly remarks,—when an old woman is concerned, Sheridan's fine gentlemen always forget their manners,— is revealed in all her poverty and ugliness beside the pretty young ladies; and Isaac's conceit and admiration of himself, "a sly little villain, a cunning dog," etc., are unmercifully laughed at; while the rest of the party make up matters with the easily mollified papa.

Such is the story: there is very little character attempted, save in Isaac, who is a sort of rudimentary sketch of a too cunning knave or artful simpleton caught in his own toils; and the dialogue, if sometimes clever enough, never for a moment reaches the sparkle of the *Rivals*. "The wit of the dialogue," Moore says—using that clever mist of words with which an experienced writer hides the fact that he can find nothing to say on a certain subject—"except in one or two instances, is of that amusing kind which lies near the surface—which is produced without effort, and may be enjoyed without wonder." If this means that there is nothing at all wonderful about it, it is no doubt true enough—though there are one or two phrases which are worth preserving, such as that in which the Jew is described as being "like the blank leaves between the Old and New Testament," since he is a convert of recent date and no very certain faith.

It was, however, the music which made the piece popular, and the songs which Sheridan wrote for Linley's setting were many of them pretty, and all neat and clever. Everybody knows "Had I a heart for falsehood framed," which is sung by the walking gentleman of the piece, a certain Don Carlos, who has nothing to do but to take care of Louisa during her wanderings, and to sing some of the prettiest songs. Perhaps on the whole this is the best :—

> " Had I a heart for falsehood framed,
>   I ne'er could injure you ;
> For though your tongue no promise claim'd
>   Your charms would make me true.
> To you no soul shall bear deceit,
>   No stranger offer wrong ;
> But friends in all the aged you'll meet,
>   And lovers in the young.
>
> " But when they learn that you have blest
>   Another with your heart,
> They'll bid aspiring passion cease
>   And act a brother's part.
> Then, lady, dread not here deceit,
>   Nor fear to suffer wrong ;
> For friends in all the aged you'll meet,
>   And lovers in the young."

The part of Carlos is put in with Sheridan's usual indifference to construction for the sake of the music, and in order to employ a certain tenor who was a favourite

with the public, there being no possible occasion for him
so far as the dramatic action is concerned.

This is what Byron, nearly half a century after, called
"the best opera" in English, and which was lauded to
the skies in its day.   The *Beggar's Opera*, with which it
is constantly compared, has, however, much outlived it
in the general knowledge, if the galvanic and forced
resurrection given by an occasional performance can be
called life.   The songs are sung no longer, and many
who quote lines like the well-known "Sure such a pair
were never seen," are in most cases totally unaware where
they come from.   Posterity, which has so thoroughly
carried out the judgment of contemporaries in respect to
the *Rivals*, has not extended its favour to the *Duenna*.
Perhaps the attempt to conjoin spoken dialogue to any
great extent with music is never a very successful
attempt: for English opera does not seem to last.   Its
success is momentary.   Musical enthusiasts care little
for the "words," and not even so much for melody as
might be desired; and the genuine playgoer is impatient
of those interruptions to the action of a piece which has
any pretence at dramatic interest, while neither of the
conjoint Arts do their best in such a formal copartnery.
Sheridan, however, spared no pains to make the partnership successful.   He was very anxious that the composer
should be on the spot, and secure that his compositions
were done full justice to.   "Harris is extravagantly
sanguine of its success as to plot and dialogue," he
writes; "they will exert themselves to the utmost in
the scenery, etc., but I never saw any one so discon-
certed as he was at the idea of there being no one to put
them in the right way as to music."   "Dearest father,"

adds Mrs. Sheridan, "I shall have no spirits or hopes of
the opera unless we see you." The young dramatist,
however, had his ideas as to the music as well as the
literary portion of the piece, and did not submit himself
blindly to his father-in-law's experience. "The first,"
he says, "I should wish to be a pert sprightly air, for
though some of the words mayn't seem suited to it, I
should mention that they are neither of them in earnest
in what they say : Leoni (Carlos) takes it up seriously,
and I want him to show advantageously in the six lines
beginning, 'Gentle Maid.' I should tell you that he
sings nothing well but in a plaintive or pastoral style,
and his voice is such as appears to me always to be hurt
by much accompaniment. I have observed, too, that he
never gets so much applause as when he makes a cadence.
Therefore my idea is that he should make a flourish at
'Shall I grieve you.'" These instructions show how
warmly Sheridan at this period of his life interested
himself in every detail of his theatrical work. Linley,
it is said, had the good sense to follow these directions
implicitly.

The success of the *Duenna* at Covent Garden put
Garrick and his company at the rival theatre on their
mettle ; and it was wittily said that "the old woman
would be the death of the old man." Garrick chose the
moment when her son was proving so dangerous a rival
to him to resuscitate Mrs. Sheridan's play called the
Discovery, in which he himself played the chief part—a
proceeding which does not look very friendly : and as
Thomas Sheridan had been put forth by his enemies as
the great actor's rival, it might well be that there was no
very kind feeling between them. But the next chapter

in young Sheridan's life shows Garrick in so benevolent
a light that it is evident his animosity to the father, if
it existed, had no influence on his conduct to the son.
Garrick was now very near the close of his career : and
when it was understood that he meant not only to retire
from the stage, but to resign his connection with the
theatre altogether, a great commotion arose in the
theatrical world.   These were the days of patents, when
the two great theatres held a sort of monopoly, and were
safe from all rivalship except that of each other.   It was
at the end of the year 1775 that Garrick's intention of
"selling his moiety of the patent of Drury Lane Theatre"
became known : and Richard Sheridan was then in the
early flush of his success, crowding the rival theatre,
and promising a great succession of brilliant work to
come.   But it could scarcely be supposed that a young
man just emerging out of obscurity—rich, indeed, in
his first gains, and no doubt seeing before him a great
future, but yet absolutely destitute of capital—could have
been audacious enough, without some special encouragement, to think of acquiring this great but precarious
property, and launching himself upon such a venture.
How he came to think of it we are left uninformed,
but the first whisper of the chance seems to have
inflamed his mind ; and Garrick, whether or not he
actually helped him with money, as some say, was at
all events favourable to him from the beginning of
the negotiations.   He had promised that the refusal
should first be offered to Colman ; but when Colman, as
he expected, declined, it was the penniless young dramatist whom of all competitors the old actor preferred.
Sheridan had a certain amount of backing, though not

enough, as far as would appear, to lessen the extraordinary daring of the venture—his father-in-law, Linley, who it is to be supposed had in his long career laid up some money, taking part in the speculation along with a certain Dr. Ford : but both in subordination to the young man who had no money at all. Here are Sheridan's explanations of the matter addressed to his father-in-law :—

"According to his (Garrick's) demand, the whole is valued at £70,000. He appears very shy of letting his books be looked into as the test of the profits on this sum, but says it must be on its nature a purchase on speculation. However, he has promised me a rough estimate of his own of the entire receipts for the last seven years. But after all it must certainly be a purchase on speculation without money's worth having been made out. One point he solemnly avers, which is that he will never part with it under the price above-mentioned. This is all I can say on the subject until Wednesday, though I can't help adding that I think we might safely give £5000 more on this purchase than richer people. The whole valued at £70,000, the annual interest is £3500 ; while this is cleared the proprietors are safe. But I think it must be infernal management indeed that does not double it."

A few days later the matter assumes a definite shape.

" Garrick was extremely explicit, and in short we came to a final resolution ; so that if the necessary matters are made out to all our satisfactions, we may sign and seal a previous engagement within a fortnight.

" I meet him again to-morrow evening, when we are to name a day for a conveyancer on our side to meet his solicitor, Wallace. I have pitched on a Mr. Phipps, at the recommendation and by the advice of Dr. Ford. The three first steps to be taken are these,—our lawyer is to look into the titles, tenures, etc., of the house and adjoining estate, the extent and limitations of the patent, etc. ; we shall then employ a builder (I think Mr. Collins) to survey the state and repair in which the whole premises are, to which Mr. G.

entirely consents ; Mr. G. will then give us a fair and attested
estimate from his books of what the profits have been, at an
average, for these last seven years. This he has shown me
in rough, and, valuing the property at £70,000, the interest
has exceeded ten per cent.

"We should after this certainly make an interest to get
the king's promise that while the theatre is well conducted,
etc., he will grant no patent for a third, though G. seems
confident he never will. If there is any truth in professions
and appearances, G. seems likely always to continue our
friend and to give every assistance in his power.

"The method of our sharing the purchase, I should think,
may be thus—Ewart to take £10,000, you £10,000, and I
£10,000.   Dr. Ford agrees with the greatest pleasure to
embark the other £5000 ; and, if you do not choose to venture
so much, will, I daresay, share it with you. Ewart is preparing his money, and I have a certainty of my part. We
shall have a very useful ally in Dr. Ford, and my father
offers his services on our own terms. We cannot unite
Garrick to our interests too firmly ; and I am convinced his
influence will bring Leasy to our terms, if he should be ill-
advised enough to desire to interfere in what he is totally
unqualified for."

Ewart was the ever-faithful friend to whose house in
London Sheridan had taken Miss Linley, whose son had
been his second in the affair with Captain Matthews,—
a man upon whose support the Sheridan family could
always rely. But the source from which young Richard
himself got the money for his own share remains a
mystery, of which no one has yet found the solution.
"Not even to Mr. Linley," says Moore, "while entering
into all other details, does he hint at the fountainhead
from which the supply is to come," and he adds a few
somewhat commonplace reflections as to the manner
in which all Sheridan's successes had as yet been
obtained.

"There was, indeed, something mysterious and miraculous about all his acquisitions, whether in love, in learning, in wit, or in wealth. How or when his stock of knowledge was laid in nobody knew : it was as much a matter of marvel to those who never saw him read as the mode of existence of the chameleon has been to those who fancied it never eat. His advances in the heart of his mistress were, as we have seen, equally trackless and inaudible, and his triumph was the first that even his rivals knew of his love. In like manner the productions of his wit took the world by surprise, being perfected in secret till ready for display, and then seeming to break from under the cloud of his indolence in full maturity of splendour. His financial resources had no less an air of magic about them : and the mode by which he conjured up at this time the money for his first purchase into the theatre remains, as far as I can learn, still a mystery."

These remarks are somewhat foolish, to say the least, since the mystery attending the sudden successes of a young man of genius is sufficiently explained as soon as his possession of that incommunicable quality has once been established : and the triumph of a brilliant youth whose fascinating talk and social attractions were one of the features of his age, over his commonplace rivals in the heart of a susceptible girl does not even require genius to explain it. But neither genius itself nor all the personal fascination in the world can, alas ! produce when it is wanted, ten thousand pounds. The anonymous author of *Sheridan and His Times* asserts confidently that Garrick himself advanced the money, having conceived a great friendship for Sheridan, and formed a strong opinion as to his capacity to increase the reputation and success of the theatre. Of this statement, however, no proof is offered, and Moore evidently gives no credence to such a suggestion, though he notices

that it had been made. The money was procured by
some friendly help, no doubt. There were, as has been
said, only the two great theatres in these days, none of
the later crop having as yet sprung up, and each being
under the protection of a patent ; the speculation therefore was not so hazardous as it has proved to be since.
It is, however, besides the mystery about the money, a
most curious transformation to see the young idler,
lover, and man of pleasure, suddenly placed at the head
of such an undertaking, with so much responsibility
upon his shoulders, and—accustomed only to the shift-
less and hand-to-mouth living of extravagant poverty—
become at once the administrator of a considerable
revenue, and the head of a little community dependent
upon him. He had done nothing all his life except, in a
fit of inspiration of very recent date, produce a couple of
plays. But it does not seem that any doubt of his
powers crossed his mind or that of any of his associates.
"Do not flag when we come to the point," he says to his
father-in-law ; "I'll answer for it we shall see many
golden campaigns."

The stir and quickening of new energy is apparent in
all he writes. The circumstances were such as might
well quicken the steadiest pulse, for not only was he
likely to lay a foundation of fortune for himself (and his
first child had lately been born,—"a very magnificent
fellow !"), but his nearest connections on both sides were
involved, and likely to owe additional comfort and importance to the young prodigal whose own father had
disowned him, and his wife's received him with the
greatest reluctance, — a reflection which could not
but be sweet. With such hopes in his mind the

sobriety and composure with which he writes are
astonishing.

" Leasy is utterly unequal to any department in the theatre.
He has an opinion of me, and is very willing to let the whole
burden and ostensibility be taken off his shoulders. But I
certainly should not give up my time and labour (for his
superior advantage, having so much greater a share) without some conclusive advantage. Yet I should by no means
make the demand till I had shown myself equal to the
task. My father purposes to be with us but one year:
and that only to give us what advantage he can from his
experience. He certainly must be paid for his trouble, and
so certainly must you. You have experience and character
equal to the line you would undertake, and it never can
enter into anybody's head that you were to give your time,
or any part of your attention, gratis because you had a share
in the theatre. I have spoken on the subject both to Garrick and Leasy, and you will find no demur on any side to
your gaining a *certain* income from the theatre, greater I
think than you could make out of it, and in this the theatre
would be acting only for its own advantage."

The other shareholder who held the half of the property—while Sheridan, Linley, and Ford divided the
other half between them—was a Mr. Lacy: and there
seems a charming possibility of some reminiscence of the
brogue, though Sheridan probably had never been touched
by it in his own person, having left Ireland as a child—
in the mis-spelling of the name. It is impossible not to
sympathise with him in the delightful consciousness of
having proved the futility of all objections, and become
the aid and hope, instead of the detriment and burden,
of both families, which must have sweetened his own
brilliant prospects. His father evidently was now fully
reconciled and sympathetic, proud of his son, and disposed (though not without a consideration) to give him

the benefit of his experience and advice ; and Linley was
to have the chance of an income from the theatre "greater
than he could make out of it." With what sweet moist-
ure the eyes of the silenced Diva at home, the St. Cecilia
whose mouth her young husband's adoring pride had
stopped, must have glistened to think that her father,
who had done all he could to keep her Sheridan at
arm's length, was now to have his fortune made by that
injured and unappreciated hero ! She had other causes
for happiness and glory. "Your grandson," Sheridan
adds in the same letter to Linley, " astonishes everybody
by his vivacity, his talents for music and poetry, and
the most perfect integrity of mind." Everything was
now brilliant and hopeful about the young pair. The
only drawback was the uneasiness of Sheridan's position
until the business should be finally settled, between
the two theatres. "My confidential connection with
the other house," he says, "is peculiarly distressing till
I can with prudence reveal my situation, and such a
treaty, however prudently managed, cannot long be kept
secret."

The matter was settled early in the year 1776,
Sheridan being then twenty-five. Before the end of
the year troubles arose with Lacy, and it would seem
that Sheridan took the strong step of retiring from the
managership and carrying the actors along with him,
leaving the other perplexed and feeble proprietor to do
the best he could with such materials as he could pick
up. All quarrels, however, were soon made up, and
affairs proceeded amicably for some time : but Sheridan
eventually bought Lacy out at a further expenditure of
£45,000, partly obtained, it would appear, from Gar-

rick, partly by other means. The narrative is not very
clear, nor is it very important to know what squabbles
might convulse the theatre, or how the friends of Lacy
might characterise the "conceited young man," who
showed no inclination to consult a colleague of so different a calibre from himself. But it seems to be agreed
on all sides that the beginning of Sheridan's reign at
Drury was not very prosperous. Though he had shown
so much energy in his financial arrangements at the
beginning, it was not easy to get over the habits of all
his previous life, and work with the steadiness and regu-
larity of a man of business, as was needful. There was
an interval of dulness which did not carry out the hopes
very naturally formed when the young dramatist who had
twice filled the rival theatre with eager crowds and
applauses came to the head of affairs. Garrick, who had so
long been its chief attraction, was gone ; and it was a new
group of actors unfamiliar to him with whom the new
manager had to do. He remodelled for them a play
of Vanburgh's, which he called a *Trip to Scarborough*,
but which, notwithstanding all he did to it, remained still
the production of an earlier age, wanting in the refine-
ment and comparative purity which Sheridan himself
had already done so much to make popular. The Miss
Hoyden, the rustic lady whom Lord Foppington is
destined to marry, but does not, is a creature of the
species of Tony Lumpkin, though infinitely less clever
and shrewd than that delightful lout, and has no sort of
kindred with the pretty gentlewoman of Sheridan's
natural period. And the public were not specially
attracted by this *réchauffé*. In fact, after all the excitement and wonderful novelty of this astonishing **launch**

into life, the reaction was great and discouraging. Old
stock pieces of a repertory of which Garrick had been
the soul,—new contrivances of pantomime "expected to
draw all the human race to Drury," and which were rendered absolutely necessary "on account of a marvellous
preparation of the kind which is making at Covent
Garden,"—must have fallen rather flat both upon the
mind of the manager, still new and inexperienced in his
office, and of the public, which no doubt at the hands of
the author of the *Rivals*, and with the songs of the
Duenna still tingling in its ears, expected great things.
But this pause was only the *reculer pour mieux sauter*
which precedes a great effort ; for early in the next year
Sheridan rose to the full height of his genius, and the
School for Scandal blazed forth, a great Jupiter among
the minor starlights of the drama, throwing the rival
house and all its preparations altogether into the shade.

CHAPTER III.

THE " SCHOOL FOR SCANDAL."

IT was clear that a great effort was required for the advantage of Drury Lane, to make up for the blow of Garrick's withdrawal, and to justify the hopes founded upon the new management; and Mr. Lacy and the public had both reason to wonder that the head which had filled Covent Garden from pit to gallery should do nothing for the house in which all his hopes of fortune were involved. No doubt the cares of management and administration were heavy, and the previous training of Sheridan had not been such as to qualify him for continuous labour of any kind; but at the same time it was not unnatural that his partners in the undertaking should have grumbled at the long interval which elapsed before he entered the lists in his own person. It was May 1777, more than a year after his entry upon the proprietorship of Drury Lane, when the *School for Scandal* was produced, and then it was hurried into the hands of the performers piecemeal before it was finished, the last act finding its way to the theatre five days before the final production. The manuscript, Moore informs us, was issued forth in shreds and patches, there being but " one rough draft of the last

five scenes scribbled upon detached pieces of paper: while
of all the preceding acts there are numerous transcripts
scattered promiscuously through six or seven books,
with new interlineations and memoranda to each. On
the last leaf of all, which exists, just as we may suppose
it to have been despatched by him to the copyist," Moore
adds, "there is the following curious specimen of a
doxology, written hastily in the handwriting of the respec-
tive parties, at the bottom :—

> 'Finished at last ; thank God !
>
> > 'R. B. SHERIDAN.
>
> 'Amen !
>
> > 'W. HAWKINS.'"

The bearer of the latter name was the prompter, and
there is a whole history of hurry and anxiety and
confusion, a company disorganised, and an unhappy
functionary at the end of his powers, in this devout
exclamation. It is bad enough to keep the press waiting,
but a dozen or so of actors arrested in their study, and
the whole business of the theatre depending upon the
time at which a man of fashion got home from an entertainment, or saw his guests depart in the grey of the
morning, is chaos indeed. "We have heard him say,"
writes a gossiping commentator, "that he had in those
early days stolen from his bed at sunrise to prosecute his
literary labours, or after midnight, when his visitors had
departed, flown to his desk, and, at the cost of a bottle of
port, sat down to resume the work which the previous
morning in its early rising had dawned upon." The
highly polished diction of the *School for Scandal*, and the

high pressure of its keen and trenchant wit, does not look
much like the excited work of the small hours inspired by
port; but a man who is fully launched in the tide of
society, and sought on all hands to give brilliancy to the
parties of his patrons, must needs "steal a few hours from
the night." "It was the fate of Sheridan through life,"
Moore says, "and in a great degree his policy, to gain
credit for excessive indolence and carelessness." It seems
very likely that he has here hit the mark, and furnished an explanation for many of the apparently headlong feats of composition by which many authors are
believed to have distinguished themselves. There is no
policy which tells better. It is not merely an excuse for
minor faults, but an extraordinary enhancement in the
eyes of the uninstructed, of merit of all kinds. To be
able to dash off in a moment, at a sitting, what would take
the laborious plodder a week's work, is a kind of triumph
which is delightful both to the performer and spectator;
and many besides Sheridan have found it a matter of
policy to keep up such a character. The anonymous
biographer whom we have already quoted is very angry
with Moore for attempting to show that Sheridan did not
dash off his best work in this reckless way, but studied
every combination, and sharpened his sword by repeated
trials of its edge and temper. The scientific critic has
always scorned what the multitude admire, and the
fashion of our own age has so far changed that to show
an elaborate process of workmanship for any piece of
literary production, and if possible to trace its lineage to
previous works and well-defined impulses and influences,
is now the favourite object of the biographer and commentator. We confess a leaning to the primitive

method, and a preference for the Minerva springing full
armed from the brain of Jove to the goddesses more
gradually developed of scientific investigation.

But Moore's account of the growth of Sheridan's
powers, and of the steps by which he ascended to the
mastery of his art, are interesting and instructive. The
Rivals sprang into being without much thought, with that
instinctive and unerring perception of the right points
to recollect and record, which makes observation the
unconscious instrument of genius, and is so immensely
and indescribably different from mere imitation. But
the *School for Scandal*—a more elaborate performance in
every way—required a different handling. It seems to
have floated in the writer's mind from the moment when
he discovered his own powers, stimulating his invention
and his memory at once, and prompting half-a-dozen
beginnings before the right path was discovered. Now
it is one story, now another, that attracts his fancy. He
will enlist those gossiping circles which he feels by
instinct to be so serviceable for the stage, to serve the
purpose of a scheming woman and separate a pair of
lovers. Anon, departing from that idea, he will employ
them to bring about the catastrophe of a loveless marriage, in which an old husband and a young wife, the
very commonplaces of comedy, shall take a new and
original development. Two distinct stories rise in his
mind like two butterflies circling about each other, keeping him for a long time undecided which is the best for
his purpose. The first plot is one which the spectator
has now a little difficulty in tracing through the brilliant
scenes which were originally intended to carry it out,
though it is distinctly stated in the first scene between

Lady Sneerwell and Snake which still opens the comedy.
As it now stands this intimation of her ladyship's purpose
is far too important for anything that follows, and is apt
to mystify the spectator, who finds little in the after
scenes to justify it—a confusion at once explained when
we are made aware that this was the original *motif* of the
entire piece, the object of which was to separate, not
Charles Surface, but a sentimental hero called Clarimont,
Florival, and other pastoral names, from the Maria whom
he loves, and who is the ward, niece, or even step-
daughter of Lady Sneerwell, a beautiful widow and
leader of scandal, who loves him.   But while the author
is playing with this plot, and designing fragmentary
scenes in which to carry it out, the other is tugging at
his fancy—an entirely distinct idea, with a group of new
and individual characters, the old man and his wife,
the two contrasted brothers, one of whom is to have
the reputation of being her lover, while the other is the
real villain.   At first there is no connection whatever
between the two.   The *School for Scandal* proper is first
tried.   Here would seem to be the first suggestions of it,
no doubt noted down at a venture for future use without
any very definite intention, perhaps after a morning's
stroll through the crowd which surrounded the waters of
the Bath with so many bitternesses.   There are here,
the reader will perceive, no indications of character, or
even names, to serve as symbols for the Crabtrees and
Candours to come.

"The Slanderer.   *A Pump-Room Scene.*

Friendly caution to the newspapers.
It is whispered——

G

She is a constant attendant at church, and very frequently
takes Dr. M'Brawn home with her.

Mr. Worthy is very good to the girl :—for my part I
dare swear he has no ill intention.

What ! Major Wesley's Miss Montague ?

Lud, ma'am, the match is certainly broke.   No creature
knows the cause : some say a flaw in the lady's character,
and others in the gentleman's fortune.

To be sure they do say——

I hate to repeat what I hear——

She was inclined to be a little too plump before they
went——

The most intrepid blush.   I've known her complexion
stand fire for an hour together."

Whether these jottings suggested the design, or were
merely seized upon by that faculty of appropriating
"son bien où il le trouve," which is one of the privileges
of genius, it is impossible to tell ; but it will be seen that
the germ of all the highly-wrought and polished scenes
of the scandalous college is in them.   The first use to
which they were put is soon visible in the scene between
Lady Sneerwell and Snake (called Spatter in the original) which opened the uncompleted play, and still stands,
though with much less significance, at the beginning of
the actual one.   In this sketch Crabtree and Sir Benjamin Backbite appear as parties to the intrigue, the latter
being the lover of Maria, and intended to embroil her
with Clarimont, who is no gallant rake like his prototype
in the existing drama, but a piece of perfection highly
superior to the gossip,—"one of your moral fellows . . .
who has too much good nature to say a witty thing himself,
and is too ill-natured to permit it in others," and who
is as dull as virtue of this abstract type is usually represented on the stage.   To show the difference in the

workmanship, we may quote the only portion of the old sketch, which is identical in meaning with the perfected one. Lady Sneerwell and Spatter are, as in the first version, "discovered" when the curtain rises.

> "*Lady S.* The paragraphs, you say, were all inserted?
> *Spat.* They were, madam.
> *Lady S.* Did you circulate the report of Lady Brittle's intrigue with Captain Boastall?
> *Spat.* Madam, by this time Lady Brittle is the talk of half the town : and in a week will be treated as a demirep.
> *Lady S.* What have you done as to the innuendo of Miss Nicely's fondness for her own footman?
> *Spat.* 'Tis in a fair train, ma'am. I told it to my hairdresser ; he courts a milliner's girl in Pall Mall, whose mistress has a first cousin who is waiting-woman to Lady Clackit. I think in about fourteen hours it must reach Lady Clackit, and then you know the business is done.
> *Lady S.* But is that sufficient, do you think?
> *Spat.* Oh, Lud, ma'am! I'll undertake to ruin the character of the primmest prude in London with half as much. Ha, ha! Did your ladyship never hear how poor Miss Shepherd lost her lover and her character last summer at Scarborough?—this was the whole of it. One evening at Lady ——'s the conversation happened to turn on the difficulty of feeding Nova Scotia sheep in England——"

The reader will recollect the story about the sheep, which is produced at a later period in the scene, under a different name in the actual version, as are Miss Nicely and her footman. To show, however, the improvement of the artist's taste, we will place beside the less perfect essay we have just quoted the scene as it stands.

> "*Lady Sneer.* The paragraphs, you say, Mr. Snake, were all inserted?
> *Snake.* They were, madam ; and as I copied them myself in a feigned hand, there can be no suspicion whence they came.

Lady Sneer. Did you circulate the report of Lady Brittle's intrigue with Captain Boastall ?

Snake. That's in as fine a train as your ladyship could wish.   In the common course of things, I think it must reach Mrs. Clackitt's ears within four-and-twenty hours, and then you know the business is as good as done.

Lady Sneer. Why, truly Mrs. Clackitt has a very pretty talent, and a great deal of industry.

Snake. True, madam, and has been tolerably successful in her day.   To my knowledge she has been the cause of six matches being broken off, and three sons disinherited. . . . Nay, I have more than once traced her causing a *téte-à-téte* in *The Town and Country Magazine*, when the parties perhaps had never seen each other before in the course of their lives.

Lady Sneer. She certainly has talents, but her manner is gross.

Snake. 'Tis very true.   She generally designs well, has a free tongue, and a bold invention ; but her colouring is too dark, and her outlines often extravagant.   She wants that delicacy of tint and mellowness of sneer which distinguish your ladyship's scandal.

Lady Sneer. You are partial, Snake.

Snake. Not in the least ; everybody allows that Lady Sneerwell can do more with a word and a look than many can with the most laboured detail, even when they happen to have a little truth on their side to support it."

It seems needless to reproduce the dull and artificial scenes which Moore quotes by way of showing how Sheridan floundered through the mud of commonplace before he found firm footing on the ground where he achieved so brilliant a success.   They are like an artist's first experiments in design, and instructive only in that sense. Perhaps it was in the despair which is apt to seize the imagination when a young writer finds his performance so inadequate to express his idea, that Sheridan threw the whole machinery of the scandalous circle aside, and

betook himself to the construction of the other drama
which had got into his brain—the story of old Teazle
and his young wife, and of the brothers Plausible or
Pliant, or half a dozen names beside, as the fancy of
their author varies. In the first sketch, our friend Sir
Peter, that caustic and polished gentleman, is Solomon
Teazle, a retired tradesman, who maunders over Margery
his first wife, and his own folly, after getting rid of
her in encumbering himself with another : but after a
very brief interval, this beginning, altogether unsuitable
to the writer's tastes and capabilities, changes insensibly
into the more harmonious conception of the old husband
as we know him. The shopkeeper was not in Sheridan's
way. Such a *hobereau* as Bob Acres, with his apings of
fashion, might come within his limited range ; but it did
not extend to those classes which lie outside of society.
Trip and Fag and their fellows were strictly within this
circle ; they are as witty as their masters in the hands
of the dramatist, and rather more fine, as is the nature
of a gentleman's gentleman ; and even royalty itself
must be content to share the stage with these indispensable ministers and copyists. But the world beyond
was at all times a sealed book to this historian of
fashionable folly—and he was wisely inspired in throwing
over the plebeian. He seems very speedily to have
found out his mistake, for nothing more is heard of
Solomon ; and in the next fragmentary scene the
dramatist glides at once into a discussion of Lady
Teazle's extravagances, in which we have a great deal
of unmeaning detail, all cleared away like magic in the
existing scene, which is framed upon it, yet is as much
superior to it as a lively and amusing altercation can be

to the items of a lengthy account interspersed with mutual recriminations. It would appear, however, that the Teazle play was subsequent to the Sneerwell one, for there is a great deal of pointed and brilliant writing, and much that is retained almost without change, in the first adumbrations of the great scenes with Joseph Surface. "So then," says Lady Teazle in this early sketch, "you would have me sin in my own defence, and part with my virtue to preserve my reputation," an epigrammatic phrase which is retained without alteration in the final scene. Moore tells us that this sentence is "written in every direction, and without any material change in its form, over the pages of his different memorandum books." It is evident that it had caught Sheridan's fancy, and that he had favourite phrases as some people have favourite children, produced on every possible occasion and always delighted in.

How it was that Sheridan was led to amalgamate these two plays into one, we are left altogether without information. Moore's knowledge seems to have been drawn entirely from the papers put into his hands, which probably no one then living knew much about, belonging as they did to the early career of a man who had lived to be old, and abandoned altogether the walk of literature, in which he had won his early laurels. He surmises that the two-act comedy which Sheridan tells Linley is about to be put in rehearsal may have been the Teazle play : but this is mere conjecture, and we can only suppose that Sheridan had found, as he grew better acquainted with the requirements of the stage, that neither of the plots he had sketched out was enough to keep the interest of the audience ; and that in the

necessity that pressed upon him for something to fill the
stage and stop the mouths of his new company and
associates, he threw the two plots together by a sudden
inspiration, knitting the one to the other by the dazzling
links of those scandalous scenes which, to tell the
truth, have very little to do with either.   Whether he
transferred these bodily from an already polished and
completed sketch, working them into the materials
needed for his double intrigue with as little alteration of
the original fabric as possible, or if in his haste and
confidence of success he deliberately refrained from connecting them with the action of the piece, we have no
way of telling.   The daring indifference which he shows
to that supposed infallible rule of dramatic composition which ordains that every word of the dialogue
should help on the action, is edifying, and shows how
entirely independent of rule is success.   At the same
time it strikes us as curious that Sheridan did not find
it expedient to employ the evil tongues a little more
upon the group of people whose fortunes are the immediate subject of the comedy.   For instance, there is no
warrant whatever in the play for the suspicion of Charles
Surface which Sir Peter expresses at an exciting moment.   A hint of his character and impending troubles
is indeed given us, but nothing that can in the least link
his name with that of Lady Teazle—which seems a distinct inadvertence on the part of the dramatist, since there
might have been an admirable opportunity for piquing
our curiosity by a *séance* of the scandalmongers upon
the possible relations between those two gay prodigals.

The scandalous scenes, however (save the last of
them), are almost entirely without connection with the

plot. They can be detached and enjoyed separately
without any sensible loss in the reader's (or even
spectator's) mind. In themselves the management
of all the details is inimitable. The eager interchange
takes away our breath; there is no break or possibility
of pause in it. The malign suggestion, the candid astonishment, the spite which assails, and the malicious good-
nature which excuses, are all balanced to perfection,
with a spirit which never flags for a moment. And
when the veterans in the art are joined by a brilliant
and mischievous recruit in the shape of Lady Teazle,
rushing in among them in pure *gaieté de cœur*, the energy
of her young onslaught outdoes them all. The talk has
never been so brilliant, never so pitiless, as when she
joins them. She adds the gift of mimicry to all their
malice, and produces a genuine laugh even from those
murderers of their neighbours' reputations. This is
one of the side-lights, perhaps unintentional, which
keen insight throws upon human nature, showing how
mere headlong imitation and high spirits, and the determination to do whatever other people do, and a little
more, go further than the most mischievous intention.
Perhaps the author falls into his usual fault of giving
too much wit and point to the utterances of the
young wife, who is not intended to be clever; but her
sudden dash into the midst of the dowagers, and unexpected victory over them in their own line, is full of
nature. "Very well, Lady Teazle, I see you can be a
little severe," said Lady Sneerwell, expressing the astonishment of the party; while Mrs. Candour hastens to
welcome Sir Peter on his arrival with her habitual complaint that "they have been so censorious—and Lady

Teazle as bad as any one." The slanderers themselves are taken by surprise, and the indignation and horror of the husband know no bounds. There is no more successful touch in the whole composition.

Apart from these scenes, the construction of the play shows once more Sheridan's astonishing instinct for a striking situation. Two such will immediately occur to the mind of the reader, the great Screen scene, and that in which Charles Surface sells his family portraits. The first is incomparably the greater of the two, and one which has rarely been equalled on the stage. The succession of interviews, one after another, has not a word too much; nor could the most impatient audience find any sameness or repetition in the successive arrivals, each one of which adds an embarrassment to the dilemma of Joseph Surface, and helps to clear up those of his victims. As the imbroglio grows before our eyes, and every door of escape for the hypocrite is shut up, without even the common sentimental error of awakening commiseration for him, the most matter-of-fact spectator can scarcely repress, even when carried along by the interest of the story, a sensation of admiring wonder at the skill with which all these combinations are effected. It is less tragic than Tartuffe, insomuch as Orgon's profound belief, and the darker guilt of the domestic traitor, move us more deeply; and it is not terrible like the unveiling of Iago; but neither is it trivial, as the ordinary discoveries of deceitful wives and friends to which we are accustomed on the stage so generally are; and the fine art with which Sir Peter, something of an old curmudgeon in the earlier scenes, is made unexpectedly to reveal his better nature, and thus prepare the way, un-

awares, for the re-establishment of his own happiness at
the moment when it seems entirely shattered, is worthy of
the highest praise. It would no doubt have been higher
art could the dramatist have deceived his audience as
well as the personages of the play, and made us also parties in the surprise of the discovery. But this is what
no one has as yet attempted, not even Shakespeare, and
we have no right to object to Sheridan that we are in
the secret of Joseph's baseness all the time, just as we
are in the secret of Tartuffe's, and can with difficulty
understand how it is that he deceives any one.   There
remains for the comedy of the future (or the tragedy,
which, wherever the deeper chords of life are touched,
comes to very much the same thing) a still greater
achievement—that of inventing an Iago who shall deceive the audience as well as the Othello upon whom he
plays, and be found out only by us and our hero at the
same moment.   Probably, could such a thing be done, the
effect would be too great, and the indignation and horror
of the crowd, thus skilfully excited, produce a sensation
beyond that which is permissible to fiction. But Sheridan
does not deal with any tragical powers. Nothing deeper
is within his reach than the momentary touch of real
feeling with which Lady Teazle vindicates herself, and
proves her capacity for better things.   The gradual development of the situation, the unwilling agency of the
deceiver in opening the eyes and touching the heart of
the woman he hopes to seduce, and clearing the character
of the brother whom he desires to incriminate ; the confusion of his mind as one after another so many dangerous elements come together ; the chuckling malice of the
old man, eager, half to exonerate Joseph from the charge

of austerity, half to betray his secret, little suspecting
how nearly his own credit is involved; the stupefying
dismay of the disclosure;—are managed with the most
complete success. The scene is in itself a succinct drama
quite comprehensible even when detached from its context, and of the highest effectiveness. So far as morals
are concerned, it is as harmless as any equivocal situation can be. To be sure the suggestion of the little
milliner is no more savoury than the presence of Lady
Teazle is becoming to her reputation and duty; but the
utter confusion of the scheme, and the admirable and unexpected turn given to the conclusion by her genuine perception of her folly and her husband's merit, go as far as
is possible to neutralise all that is amiss in it. There had
been a temporary doubt as to whether the *Rivals* would
catch the public fancy : there was none at all about this.

The other great scene, that in which Charles Surface
sells his pictures, has qualities of a different kind. It is
less perfect and more suggestive than most of Sheridan's
work. We have to accept the favourite type of the stage
hero—the reckless, thoughtless, warmhearted, impressionable spendthrift, as willing to give as he is averse to pay,
scattering his wild oats by handfuls, wasting his life and
his means in riotous living, yet easily touched and full of
kind impulses—before we can do justice to it. This character, whatever moralists may say, always has, and probably
always will retain a favoured place in fiction. Though
we know very well that in real life dissipation does not
keep the heart soft or promote gratitude and other
generous sentiments, yet we are still willing to believe
that the riotous youth whose animal spirits carry him
away into devious paths is at bottom better than the

demure one who keeps his peccadilloes out of sight of the
world.   The eighteenth century had no doubt on the
subject.   Charles Surface is the lighthearted prodigal
whose easy vices have brought him to the point of
destruction.   Whatever grave thoughts on the subject
he may have within, he is resolute in carrying out his
gay career to the end, and ready to laugh in the face of
ruin.   A more severe taste might consider his lightheartedness swagger, and his generosity prodigality ;
but we are expected on the stage to consider such
characteristics as far more frequently conjoined with
a good heart than sobriety and decency.   The reckless
young reprobate at the lowest ebb of his fortune, ready
to throw away anything or everything, and exposing
himself hopelessly and all his follies to the rich uncle
who has come to test him, conciliates our good opinion
from the beginning by the real kindness with which
he protects "little Premium," the supposed money-
lender, from the rude pleasantries of his boon companions.   The touch of desperation which is in his
gaiety without ever finding expression in words enhances
the effect of his headlong talk and wild wit.   When his
companion Careless, to whom it is all a good joke,
complains—"Charles, I haven't a hammer ; and what's
an auctioneer without a hammer?" the master of the
ruined house clutches with a laugh at the family
pedigree, firmly and tightly encircling its roller, and
throws that to him : " Here, Careless, you shall have no
common bit of mahogany ; here's the family tree for
you, and you may knock down my ancestors with their
own pedigree," he cries.   Such a laugh raises echoes
which we wonder whether Sheridan contemplated or had

any thought of. As the prodigal rattles on with almost
too much swing and "way" upon him in the tragi-comedy
of fate, we are hurried along in the stream of his wild
gaiety with sympathy which he has no right to. The
audience is all on his side from the first word. Sir
Oliver is a weakheaded old gentleman, not at all equal
to Sir Peter, and is overcome with ludicrous ease and
rapidity; but the obstinacy of affectionate gratitude
with which the hot-headed young fellow holds by the
portrait of his benefactor, and the fine superiority with
which he puts all "little Premium's" overtures aside,
without putting on any newborn virtue or pretensions
to amendment, are in their way a masterpiece. He pre-
tends no admiration for the distant uncle, but speaks of
him as freely as of the other sacrificed ancestors. "The
little ill-looking fellow over the settee" evokes no sentiment from him. He is quite willing to draw a post-obit
upon Sir Oliver's life, and to jest at him as a little nabob
with next to no liver. But for all that, a sort of impu-
dent fidelity, a reckless gratitude, is in the ruined prodigal.
The equally reckless but more composed friend, who is
ready to abet him in all his folly with the indifference of
an unconcerned bystander, the wondering contempt of
the Jew, the concealed and somewhat maudlin emotion
of the once indignant uncle, surround the figure of
the swaggering gallant with the most felicitous background. It is far less elaborate and complicated than
the companion scene; but it is scarcely less successful.

It is a curious particular in the excellence of the
piece, however, and scarcely a commendation, we fear, in
the point of view of art, that these very striking scenes,
as well as those in which the scandalmongers hold their

amusing conclave, may all be detached from the setting
with the greatest ease and without any perceptible loss
of interest. Never was there a drama which it was so
easy to take to pieces. The screen scene in itself forms,
as we have already pointed out, a succinct and brilliant
little performance which the simplest audience could
understand; and though the others might require a
word or two of preface, they are each sufficiently perfect in themselves to admit of separation from the
context. It says a great deal for the power of the
writer that this should be consistent with the general
interest of the comedy, and that we are scarcely
conscious in the acting, of the looseness with which
it hangs together, or the independence of the different parts. Sheridan, who was not a playwright by
science but rather by accident, did not in all likelihood,
in the exuberance of his youthful strength, trouble himself with any study of the laws that regulate dramatic
composition. The unities of time and place he preserves,
indeed, because it suits him to do so; the incidents of his
pieces might all happen in a few hours for anything
we know, and with singularly little change of scene ; but
the close composition and interweaving of one part with
another, which all dramatists ought, but so very few do,
study, evidently cost him little thought. He has the
quickest eye for a situation, and knows that nothing
pleases the playgoing public so much as a strong combination and climax ; but he does not take the trouble
to rivet the links of his chain or fit them very closely
into each other. It is a wonderful tribute to his power
that, notwithstanding this looseness of construction, few
people object to allow to the *School for Scandal* the pre-

eminence accorded to it by admiring contemporaries as
being the best modern English comedy.   There is more
nature and more story in *She Stoops to Conquer ;* but
nothing so brilliant, so incisive, no such concentration of
all the forces of Art, and nothing like the sparkle of
the dialogue, the polish and ease of diction.   Goldsmith's
play, though produced only three or four years before,
is a generation older in atmosphere and sentiment; but
it is the only one which has proved a competitor with
Sheridan's great comedy, or that we can compare with
it.   To go back to Shakespeare and place these brilliant
studies of Society in the eighteenth century by the side
of that radiant world of imagination which took refuge
in the woods of Arden, or found a place in the enchanted
island, would be futile indeed.   It would be little less
foolish than to compare Sheridan's prologues and occasional verses with the *Allegro* and the *Penseroso.*   Not to
that region or near it did he ever reach.   It was not his
to sound the depths of human thought or mount to any
height of fancy.   Rosalind and Prospero were out of his
reckoning altogether; but for a lively observation of
what was going on upon the surface of life, with an
occasional step a little way—but only a little way—
beyond : and a fine instinct for that concentration of
incident and interest which make a striking dramatic
scene, nobody has excelled him, and very few indeed
reach anything like the level of his power.

This play, which the actors had begun to rehearse before
it was all written, was received by everybody connected
with the theatre with excitement and applause.   Garrick
himself, it is said, attended the rehearsals, and "was
never known on any former occasion to be more anxious

for a favourite piece." The old actor threw himself with generous warmth into the interest of the new dramatist, upon whom for the moment the glory of Drury Lane depended. Moore quotes a note from him which proves the active interest he took in the production of the new play. "A gentleman who is as mad as myself about y^e *School*," he writes, "remarked that the characters upon ye stage at ye falling of ye screen stand too long before they speak. I thought so too ye first night: he said it was ye same on ye 2nd and was remark'd by others: tho' they should be astonish'd and a little petrify'd, yet it may be carry'd to too great a length." His affectionate interest is still further proved by the Prologue, in which he speaks of Sheridan with a sort of paternal admiration.

> " Is our young bard so young to think that he
>   Can stop the full spring-tide of calumny ?
>   Knows he the world so little, and its trade ?
>   Alas ! the devil's sooner raised than laid.
>   So strong, so swift, the monster there's no gagging :
>   Cut Scandal's head off, still the tongue is wagging.
>   Proud of your smiles, once lavishly bestowed,
>   Again our young Don Quixote takes the road ;
>   To show his gratitude he draws his pen,
>   And seeks the hydra, Scandal, in his den.
>   For your applause all perils he would through—
>   He'll fight—that's write—a caballero true,
>   Till every drop of blood—that's ink—is spilt for you."

It is a ludicrous circumstance in the history that an attempt was made after Sheridan's death, and by no less strange a hand than that of his first biographer, Watkins, to question the authorship of the *School for Scandal*, which, according to this absurd story, was the composi-

tion of an anonymous young lady, who sent it to the
management of Drury Lane shortly before her death, an
event of which Sheridan took advantage to produce her
work as his own! That any reasonable creature could
be found to give vent to such a ridiculous fiction, is an
evidence of human folly and malignity more remarkable than any in the play, and laughably appropriate
as connected with it, as if Sir Benjamin Backbite had
risen from the grave to avenge himself.

It is needless to add that the popularity which has
never failed for more than a century attended the first
production of the great comedy. It brought back prosperity with a bound to the theatre, which had been
struggling in vain under Sheridan's management against,
so to speak, Sheridan himself at Covent Garden in the
shape of the *Rivals* and *Duenna*. Two years after its first
production it is noted in the books of the theatre that " the
School for Scandal damped the new pieces." Nothing could
stand against it, and the account of the nightly receipts
shows with what steadiness it continued to fill the treasury,
which had been sinking to a lower and lower ebb.

Many attempts were made at the time, and have been
made since, to show how and from whom Sheridan derived
his ideas : a more justifiable appropriation than that of the
play entire, though perhaps a still more disagreeable im-
putation, since many who would not give credit to the
suggestion of a literary crime and wholesale robbery
would not hesitate to believe the lesser accusation.
Plagiarism is vile and everywhere to be condemned ;
but it is an easy exercise of the critical faculty,
and one in which, in all generations, some of the smaller
professors of the craft find a congenial field of labour,

H

to ferret out resemblances in imaginative compositions,
which are as natural as the resemblances between
members of the same race, were it not for the invidious
suggestion that the one is a theft from the other. It
would be nearly as reasonable to say that the family air
and features of a noble house were stolen from the
ancestors of the same. It is suggested accordingly that
Joseph and Charles Surface came from *Tom Jones* and
Blifil; that Mrs. Malaprop was perhaps Mrs. Slip-slop
or perhaps a sort of hash of Miss Tabitha Bramble and
her waiting maid; and even that the amusing meetings
of the *School for Scandal* were a reflection from the
Misanthrope. There will always be some who will
take a pleasure in depreciating the originality of an
author in this way; but it is scarcely necessary, now
that Sheridan himself has become a classic, to take any
trouble in pointing out the pettiness of such criticism
so far as he is concerned. Like Molière, he took his
own where he found it, with an inalienable right to
do so which no reasonable and competent literary
tribunal would ever deny. The process by which one
idea strikes fire upon another and helps to hand the
light of imagination along the line, is a natural and
noble one, honourable to every mind which has to do
with it, and as unlike the baseness of literary robbery or
imitation as any natural growth and evolution can be.
It is, indeed, one of the finest offices of the poet to
awaken smouldering thoughts in other intelligences, and
strike off into the darkness as many varied scintilla-
tions of kindred light as the race can produce. A
curious instance of the ease with which accusations of
this sort are made, as well as of how a small slander

will extend and spread, is to be found, of all places in the
world, in the record made by Samuel Rogers of the
conversations of Charles James Fox. Sheridan, among
other appropriations, had been supposed to take the idea
of Sir Oliver's return from his own mother's novel of
Sidney Biddulph. He might for that matter have taken
it from a hundred novels, since no incident was more
hackneyed. " Thought *Sidney Biddulph* one of the best
novels of the age," Rogers reports Fox to have said ;
" Sheridan denied having read it, though the plot of his
School for Scandal was borrowed from it." Sir Peter
Teazle's ball, which, after missing Charles Surface,
" struck against a little bronze Shakespeare that stood
over the fireplace, glanced out of the window at a right
angle, and wounded the postman who was just coming
to the door with a double letter from Northamptonshire,"
was scarcely a more successful example of the amplifica-
tion of report than this. It is not to be supposed that
Fox meant any harm to his friend and sometime colleague ; but the expansion of the original statement that
the idea of the Indian uncle's return came from this
source, to the bold assertion that the plot of the *School
for Scandal* was borrowed from it, is worthy of Lady
Sneerwell herself.

The play was not published in any authorised edition
during Sheridan's lifetime, probably because it was more
to his profit, according to theatrical regulations, that it
should not be so—though Sheridan's grand statement that
he had been "nineteen years endeavouring to satisfy
himself with the style of the *School for Scandal*, and had
not succeeded," may be taken as the reason if the reader
chooses. He was sufficiently dilatory and fastidious to

have made that possible. It was, however, printed in Dublin (which was the great seat of literary piracy before the Union, when it shifted farther west), from a copy which Sheridan had sent to his sister, Mrs. Lefanu, " to be disposed of for her own advantage to the manager of the Dublin theatre." Almost immediately after its production several of the scenes were " adapted " and acted in France ; and it has since been printed not only in innumerable editions in England, but translated into every European language. Nor is there, we may say, any new play, unattended by special stimulation of adventitious interest, which is still so certain of securing " a good house."

In the same year in which this masterpiece came into being, and moved by the same necessities, Sheridan produced the last of his dramatic compositions,—a work which has perhaps occasioned more innocent amusement and cordial laughter than any other of the kind in the language, and has furnished us with more allusions and illustrations than anything else out of Shakespeare. The *Critic* is, of all Sheridan's plays, the one which has least claim to originality. Although it is no copy, nor can be accused of plagiarism, it is the climax of a series of attempts descending downwards from the Elizabethan era, when the *Knight of the Burning Pestle* was performed amid the running commentaries of the homely critics : and it could scarcely have died out of the recollection of Sheridan's audience that Fielding had over and over again made the same attempt in the previous generation. But what his predecessors had tried with different degrees of success—or failure—Sheridan accomplished triumphantly. The humours of the Rehearsal, still sufficiently novel to

himself to retain all their whimsical originality, he alone
had the power so to set upon the stage that all that is
ludicrous in dramatic representation is brought before us
—but with so much dramatic success that the criticism
becomes only a more subtle kind of applause, and in the
act of making the theatre ridiculous, he makes it doubly
attractive. This amusing paradox is carried out with
the utmost skill and boldness. In the *School for Scandal*
Sheridan had held his audience in delighted suspense in
scene after scene which had merely the faintest link of
connection with the plot of his play, and did little more
than interrupt its action. But in the new work he held
the stage for nearly half the progress of the piece by the
mere power of pointed and pungent remarks, the keen
interchanges of witty talk, the personality of three or four
individuals not sufficiently developed to be considered
as impersonations of character, and with nothing to do
but to deliver their comments upon matters of literary
interest. Rarely has a greater feat been performed on
the stage. We are told that Sir Fretful Plagiary was
intended for Cumberland, that Dangle meant somebody else, and that this it was that gave the chief interest
to the first portion of the play. But what did the multitude care about Cumberland? Should it occur to any
clever playwright of our day to produce upon the stage
a caricature of one of our poets—we humbly thank
heaven much greater personages than Cumberland — a
cultivated audience for the first two or three nights
might enjoy the travesty. But London, on the whole,
when it had once gazed at the imitated great man, would
turn away without an attempt to suppress the yawn
which displayed its indifference. No popular audience

anywhere would be moved by such an expedient,—and
only a popular audience can secure the success of a play. It
was not Cumberland : it was not the theatrical enthusiast
represented by Dangle. Nothing can be more evanescent
than successes produced by such means. And this was a
vigorous and healthy success, not an affair of the coteries.
It is all the more astonishing because the play on words
is somewhat elaborate, the speeches in many cases long-
winded, and the subjects discussed of no general human
interest.   Indeed, Mr. Puff's elaborate description of
puffing, when subjected to the test of reading, is, it must
be confessed, a little tedious : which is, of all the sins of
the stage, the most unpardonable.   Supposing any young
dramatist of the present day to carry such a piece to a
stage manager, we can imagine the consternation with
which his proposal would be received.   What ! take up
the time of the public with a discussion of literary
squabbles, and the passion of an irate author attacked
by the press !—expect the world to be amused by the pre-
sentation upon the stage even of the most caustic of
Saturday reviewers, the sharpest operator of the nineteenth century, although in the very act of baiting a playwright !   The young experimentalist would be shown
to the door with the utmost celerity.   His manuscript
would not even be unrolled—in all probability his
theatrical friend would read him a lecture upon his
utter misconception of the purposes of the stage.   " My
dear Sir," we can imagine him saying, with that mixture
of blandness and impatience with which a practical man
encounters an idealist, "there cannot be a greater mistake than to suppose that the world cares for what literary persons say of each other.   Your testy old gentle-

man might be bearable if he had a daughter to marry,
or a son to disinherit; but all this noise and fury about
a review! Tut! the audience would be bored to death."
And so any sensible adviser would say. Yet Sir Fretful
between his two tormentors, and the cheerful bustle
and assured confidence of Mr. Puff, have held their
ground when hundreds of sensational dramas have
drooped and died. Never was a more wonderful
literary feat. The art of puffing has been carried to
a perfection unsuspected by Mr. Puff, and not one person in a thousand has the most remote idea who Cumberland was,—but the *Critic* is as delightful as ever,
and we listen to the gentlemen talking with as much
relish as our grandfathers did. Nay, the simplest-minded
audience, innocent of literature, and perhaps not very
sure what it all means, will still answer to the touch,
and laugh till they cry over the poor author's wounded
vanity and the woes of Tilburina. Shakespeare, it is
evident, found the machinery cumbrous, and gave up
the idea of making Sly and his mockers watch the progress of the *Taming of the Shrew*, and Beaumont and
Fletcher lose our interest altogether in their long-drawn-
out by-play though the first idea of it is comical in
the highest degree. Nor could Fielding keep the stage
with his oft-repeated efforts, notwithstanding the wit
and point of many of his dialogues. But Sheridan at
last, after so many attempts, found out the right vein.
It is evident by the essays made in his own boyhood that
the subject had attracted him from a very early period.
His lively satire, keen as lightning, but harmless as the
flashing of the summer storm which has no thunder in
it, finds out every crevice in the theatrical mail. When

he has turned the author outside in, and exposed all his
little weaknesses (not without a sharper touch here, for it
is Mr. Puff the inventor of the art of advertising as it
was in those undeveloped days, and not any better man
who fills the place of the successful dramatist), he turns
to the play itself with the same delightful perception of
its absurdities. The bits of dialogue which are interposed
sparkle like diamonds.

> " *Sneer.* Pray, Mr. Puff, how came Sir Christopher Hatton
> never to ask that question before ?
> *Puff.* What, before the play began ?—how the plague
> could he ?
> *Dangle.* That's true, i'faith !"

And again—

> " *Dangle.* Mr. Puff, as he knows all this, why does Sir
> Walter go on telling him ?
> *Puff.* But the audience are not supposed to know any-
> thing of the matter, are they ?
> *Sneer.* True ; but I think you manage ill : for there cer-
> tainly appears no reason why Sir Walter should be so com-
> municative.
> *Puff.* 'Fore Gad, now, that is one of the most ungrateful
> observations I ever heard !—for the less inducement he has
> to tell all this, the more I think you ought to be obliged to
> him, for I'm sure you'd know nothing of the matter without it.
> *Dangle.* That's very true, upon my word."

In these interpolations every word tells ; but there
is no malice in the laughing champion who strikes so full
in the centre of the shield, and gets such irresistible
fooling out of the difficulties of his own art. It is
amusing to remember, though Leigh Hunt in his somewhat shrill and bitter sketch of Sheridan points it out with
unfriendly zeal, that the sentimental dramas which he

afterwards prepared for the stage were of the very order
which he here exposed to the laughter of the world.
"It is observable, and not a little edifying to observe,"
says this critic, "that when those who excel in a spirit
of satire above everything else come to attempt serious
specimens of the poetry and romance whose exaggera-
tions they ridicule, they make ridiculous mistakes of
their own and of the very same kind: *so allied is habitual
want of faith with want of all higher power.* The style of
the *Stranger* is poor and pick-thank enough; but *Pizarro*
in its highest flights is downright booth at a fair—a
tall spouting gentleman in tinsel." The words in italics
are worthy of Joseph Surface. But the more sympathetic reader will be glad to remember that *Pizarro* has
passed out of the recollection of the world so completely
that no one but a biographer or unfriendly critic would
ever think nowadays of associating it with Sheridan's
name. "Serious specimens of poetry and romance"
were entirely out of his way. The most extravagant of
his admirers has never claimed for him any kindred with
the Shakespearian largeness which makes Lear and
Touchstone members of the same vast family. That
Sheridan himself, when driven to it, fell into the lowest
depths of dramatic bathos need not injure our appreciation of his delightful and lighthearted mockery and
exposure of all its false effects. In the *Critic* he is at the
height of his powers; his keen sense of the ridiculous
might have, though we do not claim it for him, a moral aim,
and be directed to the reformation of the theatre ; but his
first inspiration came from his own enjoyment of the
humours of the stage and perception of its whimsical
incongruities. No doubt, however, he was weighed

down by the preposterous dramas which were submitted to him for the use of the company at Drury Lane,
when he broke forth into this brilliant piece of fun and
mockery. It afforded a most useful lesson to the drama-
tical writers then abusing their prerogative and filling the
stage with bathos and highflown folly ; and there is no
reason why we should refuse to Sheridan the credit of a
good purpose, as well as of a most amusing and in no
way ill-natured extravaganza, admirably true, so far as it
goes, and skimming the surface of society and of some
developments of human nature with an unerring hand.

Another of the many strange anecdotes told of Sheridan's dilatoriness and headlong race against time at the
end, is connected with the composition of the *Critic*. It
is perfectly in keeping with his character, but it must
not be forgotten that it was his policy to suffer such
tales to be current, and even to give them a certain
amount of justification. The *Critic* was announced and
talked of long before its completion, nay, before it was
begun—not a singular event perhaps in dramatic experience. It was then sent to the theatre in detached
scenes, as had been the case with the *School for Scandal*.
Finally a definite date was fixed for its appearance—the
30th of October ; but when the 27th had arrived, the
work, to the despair of everybody connected with the
theatre, was still incomplete.

We quote from *Sheridaniana*, an anonymous publication
intended to make up the deficiencies of Moore's life, the
following account of the amusing expedient by which
the conclusion was accomplished.

"Dr. Ford and Mr. Linley, the joint proprietors, began to get
nervous and uneasy, and the actors were absolutely *au désespoir*,

especially King, who was not only stage-manager, but had to play Puff. To him was assigned the duty of hunting down and worrying Sheridan about the last scene ; day after day passed, until the last day but two arrived, and still it did not make its appearance. At last Mr. Linley, who, being his father-in-law, was pretty well aware of his habits, hit upon a stratagem. A night rehearsal of the *Critic* was ordered, and Sheridan having dined with Linley was prevailed upon to go. When they were on the stage, King whispered to Sheridan that he had something particular to communicate, and begged he would step into the second greenroom. Accordingly Sheridan went, and found there a table with pens, ink, and paper, a good fire, an armchair at the table, and two bottles of claret, with a dish of anchovy sandwiches. The moment he got into the room, King stepped out and locked the door ; immediately after which Linley and Ford came up and told the author that until he had written the scene he would be kept where he was. Sheridan took this decided measure in good part : he ate the anchovies, finished the claret, wrote the scene, and laughed heartily at the ingenuity of the contrivance."

We have the less compunction in quoting an anecdote, vouched for only by anonymous witnesses, that there can be little doubt it was a kind of story which Sheridan would have given no contradiction to. The dash of sudden creation making up for long neglect of duty was the conventional mode of procedure for such a man. To discuss the immorality of such a mode of action would be altogether out of place here. Every evasion of duty is due to some sort of selfishness; but the world has always been indulgent (up to a certain point) of the indolent and vagrant character which is conjoined with a capacity for great work in an emergency, and, so long as the thing is done, and done with such brilliancy at last, will condone any irregularity in the doing of it.

The result, it is said, of the *Critic* was immediately apparent. For some time after its production the old type of tragedy became impossible, at least at Drury Lane. Dramas in which "the heroine was found to be forestalled by Tilburina," could not be any great loss to the stage ; and it is amusing to realise the aspect of an audience fresh from the *Critic*, when such a tragedy was placed on the boards, while the spectators vainly struggled to shut out a recollection of the Governor opposing his honour to all the seductions of his daughter, or Whiskerandos refusing to die again on any entreaty, from their minds. It was little wonder if all the craft were furious, and the authors—whose productions were chased by laughter from the stage—could not find any abuse bitter enough for Sheridan.

There was, unfortunately, very good cause for complaint on other grounds. To speak of his habits of business as being bad would be absurd, for he had no business habits at all. His management of the theatre when it fell into his hands was as discreditable as could be. He allowed everything to go to confusion, and letters and the manuscripts submitted to him, and every application relating to the theatre, to accumulate, till even the cheques for which he sent to his treasury, and which he had a thousand uses for, were confounded in the general heap and lost to him, till some recurring incident or importunate applicant made an examination of these stores a necessity. It is somewhat difficult to make out how far and how long, or if ever, he was himself responsible for the stage-management; but all the business of the theatre went to confusion in his hands, and it would appear that at first at least the company took

example by the disorderly behaviour of their head.
Garrick, who had hoped so highly from the new proprietor and done so much for him, had to apologise as
he could for a state of things which looked like chaos
come again. "Everybody is raving against Sheridan
for his supineness," cries one of Garrick's correspondents;
and the unfortunate Hawkins, the prompter whose Amen
upon the end of the manuscript we have described, affords
us a picture of the kingdom of misrule which existed at
Drury Lane which is pitiful enough:

"We played last night *Much Ado About Nothing*," (writes
this martyr), "and had to make an apology for the three
principal parts. About twelve o'clock Mr. Henderson sent
word that he was not able to play. We got Mr. Louis from
Covent Garden, who supplied the part of Benedick. Soon
after, Mr. Parsons sent word he could not play. Mr. Moody
supplied the part of Dogberry; and about four in the after-
noon Mr. Vernon sent word he could not play. Mr. Mat-
tock supplied his part of Balthazar. I thought myself very
happy in getting these wide gaps so well stopped. In the
middle of the first act a message was brought to me that Mr.
Lamash, who was to play the part of Borachio, was not come
to the house. I had nobody then who could go on for it, so
I was obliged to cut two scenes in the first and second act
entirely out, and get Mr. Wrighton to go on for the remainder
of the piece. At length we got the play over without the
audience finding it out. We had a very bad house. Mr.
Parsons is not able to play in the *School for Scandal* to-morrow
night: do not know how we shall be able to settle that. I
hope the pantomime may prove successful, and release us
from this dreadful situation."

This was the condition into which the orderly and
well-governed theatre had fallen soon after Garrick resigned into Sheridan's younger, and, as he hoped, better
hands—the young Hercules who was to succeed old

Atlas in carrying the weight of the great undertaking
on his shoulders, his kingdom and authority. The receipts, that infallible thermometer of theatrical success,
soon began to fail, and everything threatened destruction,
which was averted violently by the production one after
the other of Sheridan's two plays, only to fall back into
wilder chaos afterwards. For some part of this time
the elder Sheridan, who, after their reconciliation, had
engaged with his son as one of the members of the
company, was stage manager. It is pleasant to see the
claims of nature thus acknowledged, and to have this
practical proof that Sheridan still believed in his father's
talents and capabilities : but it does not seem to have
been a fortunate attempt.   Thomas Sheridan is said to
have been as harsh as his son was easy and disorderly.
His highest effort in his profession had been made in the
hope of rivalling the great actor, with whose name and
fame and all the traditions of his method Drury Lane
was filled.   He was an elocutionist, and believed salvation to depend upon a certain measure of delivery which
he had himself invented and perfected, and concerning
which he was at once an enthusiast and a pedant.   To
introduce such a man to the little despotism of a theatre,
and set him over the members of an opposite faction in
his art, was, even when tempered by the mildness of
Linley, a desperate expedient, and his reign did not last
very long. Whether it returned to Sheridan's own shift-
less hands before a more competent head was found, it
is difficult to make out ; but at all events it was long
enough under his disorderly sway to turn everything upside down.   The ridiculous story referred to
above about the authorship of the *School for Scandal* was

supported by the complaints of authors whose manuscript dramas had never been returned to them, and to
whom it was easy to say that Sheridan had stolen their
best ideas and made use of them as his own. A portion
of one of the first scenes in the *Critic* which is now out
of date, and which indeed many people may read without any real understanding of what it refers to, makes
special reference to complaints and animadversions of
this kind. Sir Fretful announces that he has sent his
play to Covent Garden :—

" *Sneer.* I should have thought now it would have been
better cast (as the actors call it) at Drury Lane.

Sir Fret. Oh lud, no ! never send a play there while I
live.   Hark'ye [*Whispers Sneer*].

Sneer. Writes himself ! I know he does——

Sir Fret. I say nothing.   I take away from no man's
merit, am hurt at no man's good fortune.   I say nothing.
But this I will say : through all my knowledge of life I have
observed that there is not a passion so strongly rooted in the
human heart as envy.

Sneer. I believe you have reason for what you say, indeed.

Sir Fret. Besides—I can tell you it is not always safe to
leave a play in the hands of those who write themselves.

Sneer. What ! they may steal from them, my dear
Plagiary.

Sir Fret. Steal ! to be sure they may ; and egad ! serve
your best thoughts as gipsies do stolen children, disfigure
them to make them pass for their own——

Sneer. But your present work is a sacrifice to Melpomene,
and he, you know——

Sir Fret. That's no security : a dexterous plagiarist may
do anything.   Why, sir, for aught I know, he might take out
some of the best things in my tragedy and put them into his
own comedy."

Thus it is apparent Sheridan himself was perfectly

conscious of the things that were said about him. He
gave no contradiction, it is said, to the absurd story
about the *School for Scandal*—how should he ? To such
an extraordinary accusation a contemptuous silence was
the best answer. But it is with an easy good-humour,
a laugh of the most cheerful mockery, that he confronts
the bitter gossip which suggests the unsafeness of leaving
manuscripts in his hands. He was not himself ashamed
of his sins in this respect. His bag of letters all jumbled
together, his table covered with papers, the suitors who
waited in vain for a hearing, the business that was done
by fits and starts in the interval of his other engagements,—all this did not affect his conscience. Cumberland, as if to prove his identity with Sheridan's sketch,
describes in a letter to Garrick the ways of the new
manager ; and the reader will see by this brief paragraph how like was the portrait. "I read," said the
dramatist, " the tragedy in the ears of the performers on
Friday morning. I was highly flattered by the audience,
but your successor in the management is not a representative of your polite attention to authors on such occasions, for he came in yawning at the fifth act with no
other apology than having sat up two nights running.
It gave me not the slightest offence, as I put it all to the
habit of dissipation and indolence : but I fear his office
will suffer from want of due attention," Sir Fretful adds.
   This was within a few years of Sheridan's entry upon
the property and responsibility of the theatre. All that
he possessed—which means all that he had by miraculous
luck and by mysterious means, which no one has ever
been able to fathom, scraped together—was embarked in
it. It had enabled him to euter at once upon a way of

living, and into a sphere of society in which the son of the
needy player and lecturer, the idle youth of Bath, without
a profession or a penny,—the rash lover who had married
without the most distant prospect of being able to maintain his wife, yet haughtily forbidden her to exercise her
profession and maintain him,—could never have expected
to find himself. If ever man had an inducement to
devote himself to the cultivation of the extraordinary
opportunities which had been thus given to him, it was
he. But he had never been trained to devote himself to
anything, and the prodigality of good fortune which had
fallen upon him turned his head, and made him believe
no doubt that everything was to be as easy as the
beginning. Garrick had made a great fortune from the
theatre, and there was every reason to expect that Sheridan,
so easily proved the most successful dramatist of his day,
might do still more. But Sheridan, alas! had none of
the qualities which were requisite for this achievement;
even in composition he had soon reached the length of his
tether. Twice he was able to make up brilliantly by an
almost momentary effort for the bad effects of his carelessness in every practical way. But it is not possible for
any man to go on doing this for ever, and the limit of
his powers was very soon reached. If he had kept to
his own easy trade and sphere, and refrained from public
life and all its absorbing cares, would he have continued
periodically to remake his own fortune and that of the
theatre by a new play? Who can tell? It is always
open to the spectator to believe that such might have
been the case, and that Sheridan, put into harness like
a few greater spirits, might have maintained an endless stream of production as Shakespeare did. But

I

there are indications of another kind which may lead
critics to decide differently.   Sheridan's view of life
was not a profound one.   It was but a vulgar sort of
drama, a problem without any depths—to be solved by
plenty of money and wine and pleasure, by youth and
high spirits, and an easy lavishness which was called
liberality, or even generosity as occasion served.   But
to Sheridan there was nothing to find out in it, any more
than there is anything to find out in the characters of
his plays.   He had nothing to say further.   Lady Teazle's
easy penitence, her husband's pardon, achieved by the
elegant turn of her head seen through the open door,
and the entry of Charles Surface into all the good
things of this life, in recompense for an insolent sort
of condescending gratitude to his egotistical old uncle,
were all he knew on this great subject.   And when
that was said he had turned round upon the stage, the
audience, the actors, and the writers who catered for
them, and made fun of them all with the broadest mirth,
and easy indifference to what might come after.   What
was there more for him to say ?   The *Critic*, so far as the
impulse of creative energy, or what, for want of a better
word, we call genius, was concerned, was Sheridan's last
word.

It was during this period of lawlessness and misrule
at Drury, while either Sheridan himself or his father
was holding the sceptre of unreason there, that Garrick
died.   He had retired from the theatre only a few years
before, and had watched it with anxious interest ever
since, no doubt deeply disappointed by the failure of
the hopes which he had founded upon the new proprietorship and the brilliant young substitute whom

he had helped to put into his own place. Sheridan
followed him to the grave as chief mourner—and his
impressionable nature being strongly touched by the
death of the man who had been so good to him, shut
himself up for a day or two, and wrote a monody to
Garrick's memory, which met with much applause in its
day. It was seemly that some tribute should be paid
to the great actor's name in the theatre of which he had
for so long been the life and soul, though Sheridan's
production of his own poem at the end of the play
which was then running, as an independent performance
and sacrifice to the *manes* of his predecessor was a novelty
on the stage. It was partly said and partly sung, and
must have been on the whole a curious interlude in its
solemnity amid the bustle and animation of the evening's
performance. As a poem it is not remarkable, but it is
the most considerable of Sheridan's productions in that
way. The most characteristic point in it is the complaint of the evanescence of an actor's fame and reputation, which was very appropriate to the moment, though
perhaps too solemn for the occasion. After recording
the honours paid to the poet and painter, he contrasts
their lasting fame with the temporary reputation of the
heroes of the stage.

> " The actor only shrinks from time's award ;
>   Feeble tradition is his mem'ry's guard ;
>   By whose faint breath his merits must abide,
>   Unvouch'd by proof—to substance unallied !
>   E'en matchless Garrick's art to heaven resign'd,
>   No fix'd effect, no model leaves behind !
>   The grace of action, the adapted mien,
>   Faithful as nature to the varied scene ;
>   The expressive glance whose subtle comment draws

Entranced attention and a mute applause ;
Gesture which marks with force and feeling fraught,
A sense in silence and a will in thought ;
Harmonious speech whose pure and liquid tone
Gives verse a music scarce confess'd its own.

.   .   .   .   .

All perishable ! like th' electric fire,
But strike the frame—and as they strike expire ;
Incense too pure a bodied flame to bear,
Its fragrance charms the sense and blends with air.
Where then—while sunk in cold decay he lies,
And pale eclipse for ever seals those eyes—
Where is the blest memorial that ensures
Our Garrick's fame ? Whose is the trust ?—'tis yours !"

No one would grudge Garrick all the honour that
could be paid him on the stage where he had been so
important a figure.   But that the fame of the actor
should be like incense which melts in the air and dies is
very natural, notwithstanding Sheridan's protest.   The
poetry which inspires him is not his, nor the sentiments to which he gives expression.   He is but an
interpreter; he has no claim of originality upon our
admiration.   But Garrick, if any man, has had a
reputation of the permanent kind.   His name is as
well known as that of Pope or Samuel Johnson.   His
generation, and the many notable persons in it, gave him
a sort of worship in his day.   He was buried in Westminster Abbey, his pall borne by noble peers, thirty-
four mourning coaches in all the panoply of woe following, " while the streets were lined with groups of
spectators falling in with the train as it reached the
Abbey."   And up to this day we have not forgotten
Garrick.   He died in 1779, just four years after the
beginning of Sheridan's connection with the theatre.

The Monody came in between the *School for Scandal*
and the *Critic*, the keenest satire and laughter alternating
with the dirge, which, however, was only permitted for a
few nights—the audience in general have something else
to do than to amuse itself by weeping over the lost.

It must have been shortly after this solemn performance that the theatre found a more suitable manager in
the person of King the actor: and though Sheridan
never ceased to harass and drain it, yet the business of
every day began to go on in a more regular manner.
His father retired from the head of the affairs, and he
had fortunately too much to do cultivating pleasure and
society to attempt this additional work,—even with the
assistance of his Betsey, who seems to have done him
faithful service through all these early years.   He was
still but twenty-nine when his growing acquaintance with
statesmen and interest in political affairs opened to the
brilliant young man, whom everybody admired, the
portals of a more important world.

CHAPTER IV.

PUBLIC LIFE.

WHILE Sheridan was completing his brief career in literature, and bringing fortune and fame to one theatre after another by the short series of plays, each an essay of a distinct kind in dramatic composition, which we have discussed, his position had been gradually changing. It had been from the beginning, according to all rules of reason, a perfectly untenable position. When he established himself in London with his beautiful young wife they had neither means nor prospects to justify the life which they immediately began to lead, making their house, which had no feasible means of support, into a sort of little social centre, and collecting about it a crowd of acquaintances much better off than they, out of that indefinite mass of society which is always ready to go where good talk and good music are to be had, to amuse themselves at the cost of the rash entertainers, who probably believe they are "making friends" when they expend all their best gifts upon an unscrupulous, though fashionable, mob. Nothing could be more unwarrantable than this outset upon an existence which was serious to neither of them, and in which

wit and song were made the servants of a vague and
shifting public which took everything and gave nothing.
Society (in words) judges leniently the foolish victims
who thus immolate themselves for its pleasure, giving
them credit for generosity and other liberal virtues : but
it is to be feared that the excitement of high animal spirits
and the love of commotion and applause have more to
do with their folly than kindness for their fellow-crea-
tures. The two young Sheridans had both been brought
up in an atmosphere of publicity, and to both of them
an admiring audience was a sort of necessity of nature.
And it is so easy to believe, and far easier then than now,
that to "make good friends" is to make your fortune.
Sheridan was more fortunate than it is good for our
moral to admit any man to be. His rashness, joined to
his brilliant social qualities, seemed at first—even before
dramatic fame came in to make assurance sure—likely
to attain the reward for which he hoped, and to bring
the world to his feet. But such success, if for the
moment both brilliant and sweet, has a Nemesis from
whose clutches few escape.

It is evident that there were some connections of his
boyish days, Harrow schoolfellows, who had not forgotten
him, or were ready enough to resume old acquaintance—
and gay companions of the holiday period of Bath, among
whom was no less a person than Windham—who helped
him to the friendship of others still more desirable.
Lord John Townshend, one of these early friends,
brought him acquainted with the most intimate and distinguished of his after associates—the leader with whom
the most important part of his life was identified. It
was thus that he formed the friendship of Fox.

"I made (Townshend writes) the first dinner-party at
which they met, having told Fox that all the notions he
might have conceived of Sheridan's talents and genius from
the comedy of *The Rivals*, etc., would fall infinitely short of
the admiration of his astonishing powers which I was sure
he would entertain at the first interview. The first interview between them — there were very few present, only
Tickell and myself, and one or two more — I shall never
forget. Fox told me after breaking up from dinner that he
always thought Hare, after my uncle Charles Townshend,
the wittiest man he ever met with, but that Sheridan surpassed them both infinitely : and Sheridan told me next
day that he was quite lost in admiration of Fox, and that
it was a puzzle to him to say what he admired most, his
commanding superiority of talent and universal knowledge,
or his playful fancy, artless manners, and benevolence of
heart, which showed itself in every word he uttered."

At very nearly the same time Sheridan became
acquainted with Burke. Dr. Johnson himself, it is said,
proposed him as a member of the Literary Club, and his
friendship and connection with Garrick must have introduced him widely among the people whom it is distinction
to know. "An evening at Sheridan's is worth a week's
waiting for," Fox is reported to have said. The brilliant
young man with his lovely wife was such a representative of genius as might have dazzled the wisest. He
had already made the most brilliant beginning, and who
could tell what he might live to do with the world still
before him, vigorous health and undaunted spirits, and
all the charm of personal fascination to enhance those
undeniable powers which must have appeared far greater
then, in the glow of expectation, and lustre of all they
were yet to do, than we know them now to have been?
And when he stepped at once from the life, without
any visible means, which he had been living, to the posi-

tion of proprietor of Drury Lane, with an established occupation and the prospect of certain fortune, there seemed nothing beyond his legitimate ambition, as there was nothing beyond his luxury and hospitality, and lavish enjoyment. Social success so great and rapid is always rare, and the contrast between the former life of the poor player's penniless son, walking the streets of Bath in idleness without a sixpence in his pocket, and that of the distinguished young dramatist on the edge of public life, making a close alliance with two of the first statesmen of the day, invited everywhere, courted everywhere, must have been overwhelming. If his head had been turned by it, and the head of his Eliza (or his Betsey as he calls her with magnanimous disdain of finery), who could have been surprised? That his foundations were altogether insecure, and the whole fabric dangerous and apt to topple over like a house of cards, was not an idea which, in the excitement of early triumph, he was likely to dwell upon.

He had, as is evident from the scattered fragments which Moore has been careful to gather up, a fancy for politics and discussion of public matters at an early period, and intended to have collected and published various essays on such subjects shortly after his marriage. At least it is supposed that the solemn announcement made to Linley of "a book" on which he had been "very seriously at work," which he was just then sending to the press, "and which I think will do me some credit if it leads to nothing else," must have meant a collection of these papers. Nothing more was ever heard of it so far as appears; but they were found by his biographer among the chaos of scraps and uncompleted work through which he had to wade. Among these, Moore says, "are a few political letters, evidently designed for the newspapers, some of them but half copied out, and probably never sent, . . ." and "some commencements of periodical papers under various names, *The Dictator*, *The Dramatic Censor*, etc., none of them apparently carried beyond the middle of the first number;" among which, oddly enough, — a strange subject for Captain Absolute to take in hand, — "is a letter to the Queen recommending the establishment of an institution for the instruction and maintenance of young females in the better classes of life, who, from either the loss of their parents or poverty, are without the means of being brought up suitably to their station," to be founded on the model of St. Cyr, placed under the patronage of Her Majesty, and entitled "The Royal Sanctuary." This fine scheme is supported by eloquence thoroughly appropriate at once to the subject in such hands, and to the age of the writer. "The dispute about the proper sphere of women is idle," he says. "That men should have attempted to draw a line for their orbit shows that God meant them for comets, and above our jurisdiction. With them the enthusiasm of poetry and idolatry of love is the simple voice of nature." . . . "How can we be better employed," the young man adds with a lofty inspiration which puts all modern agitations on the subject to shame, "than in perfecting that which governs us? The brighter they are the more shall we be illumined. Were the minds of all women cultivated by inspiration men would become wiser of course. They are a sort of pentagraphs with which nature writes on the heart of man: what she delineates on the original

map will appear on the copy." This fine contribution
to the literature of a subject which has taken so important a place among the discussions of to-day would perhaps, however, scarcely accord with the tone of the arguments now in use.

From this romantic question he diverged into politics
proper; and under the stimulation of London life, and
his encounter with the actual warriors of the day, the
tide had begun to run so strongly that Sheridan ven-
tured an unwary stroke against the shield which Dr.
Johnson had just hung up against all comers in his
pamphlet on the American question. Fortunately for
himself it did not come to anything, for he had intended, it appears, to instance Johnson's partisanship on
this occasion as a proof of the effect of a pension, describ-
ing "such pamphlets" as "trifling and insincere as the
venal quit-rent of a birthday ode," and stigmatising the
great writer himself, the Autocrat of the past age, as
"an eleemosynary politician who writes on the subject
merely because he has been recommended for writing
otherwise all his lifetime." Such profanity will make
the reader shiver : but fortunately it never saw the light,
and with easy levity the young dramatist turned round
and paid the literary patriarch such a compliment upon
the stage as perhaps the secret assault made all the
warmer. This was conveyed in a prologue written
by Sheridan to a play of Savage :—

> " So pleads the tale that gives to future times
> The son's misfortunes and the parent's crimes ;
> There shall his fame if own'd to-night survive,
> Fix'd by the hand that bids our language live."

Another political essay of a less personal character

upon the subject of Absenteeism in Ireland also forms
one of these unfinished relics. Sheridan was so little of
an Irishman in fact that there is not, we think, a single
trace even of a visit to his native country from the time
he left it as a child, and all his personal interests and
associations were in England. But his family had veered
back again to the place of their birth, his brother
and sisters having settled in Dublin, and no doubt a
warmer interest than the common would naturally be in
the mind of a man whose veins were warmed by that
sunshine which somehow gets into English blood on the
other side of the narrow seas. In those elementary
days when Ireland was but beginning to find out that
her woes could have a remedy, Absenteeism was the
first and greatest of the evils that were supposed to
oppress her, and the optimists of the period were disposed to believe that could her landlords be persuaded
to reside on their estates, all would be well. The
changed ideas and extraordinary development of requirements since that simple age make it interesting
to quote Sheridan's view of the situation then. He
sets before us the system which we at present identify
with the tactics rather of Scotch than of Irish landlords,
that of sacrificing the people to sheep (since followed by
deer), and substituting large sheep farms for the smaller
holdings of the crofters or cotters, with considerable
force, although argument on that side of the question
has gone so much further and sustained so many changes
since then.

"It must ever be the interest of the Absentee to place
his estate in the hands of as few tenants as possible, by
which means there will be less difficulty or hazard in col-

lecting his rents and less entrusted to an agent, if the estate require one. The easiest method of effecting this is by laying out the land for pasturage, and letting it in grass to those who deal only in a ' fatal living crop,' whose produce we are not allowed a market for where manufactured, while we want art, honesty, and encouragement to fit it for home consumption. Thus the indolent extravagance of the lord becomes subservient to the interests of a few mercenary graziers— shepherds of most unpastoral principles—while the veteran husbandman may lean on the shattered unused plough and view himself surrounded with flocks that furnish raiment without food. Or if his honesty be not proof against the hard assaults of penury, he may be led to revenge himself on those ducal innovators of his little field—then learn too late that some portion of the soil is reserved for a crop more fatal even than that which tempted and destroyed him.

"Without dwelling on the particular ill effects of non-residence in this case, I shall conclude with representing that powerful and supreme prerogative which the Absentee foregoes—the prerogative of mercy, of charity. The estated resident is invested with a kind of relieving providence—a power to heal the wounds of undeserved misfortune, to break the blows of adverse fortune, and leave chance no power to undo the hopes of honest persevering industry. There cannot surely be a more happy station than that wherein prosperity and worldly interest are to be best forwarded by an exertion of the most endearing offices of humanity. This is his situation who lives on the soil which furnishes him with means to live. It is his interest to watch the devastation of the storm, the ravage of the flood, to mark the pernicious extremes of the elements, and by a judicious indulgence and assistance to convert the sorrows and repinings of the sufferer into blessings on his humanity. By such a conduct he saves his people from the sin of unrighteous murmurs, and makes heaven his debtor for their resignation."

It is strange yet not incomprehensible that the course of events should have turned this plaint and appeal to the landlords to unite themselves more closely with their tenants into the present fierce endeavour to get rid of landlords altogether. In the end of last century everybody repeated the outcry. It was the subject of Miss Edgeworth's popular stories, as well as of young Sheridan's first essay in political writing. Perhaps, had the appeal been cordially responded to in these days, there would have been a less dangerous situation, a milder demand, in our own.

These not very brilliant but sensible pages were the first serious attempts of Sheridan, so far as appears, to put together his thoughts upon a political subject. He had shown no particular inclination towards public life in his earlier days : no resort to debating clubs, like that which at a later period brought Canning under the eyes of those in power, is recorded of him. Oratory in all probability had been made odious to him by his father's unceasing devotion to his system, and the prominence which the art of elocution had been made to bear in his early life. And it is a little difficult to make out how it was that, just as he had achieved brilliant success in one career he should have so abruptly turned to another, and set his heart and hopes on that in preference to every other path to distinction. No doubt a secret sense that in this great sphere there were superior triumphs to be won must have been in his mind. Nobody, so far as we are aware, has ever doubted Sheridan's honesty or the sincerity of his political opinions. At the same time it can scarcely be imagined that the acquaintance of Fox and Burke had not a large share in determining these opinions, and that other hopes and wishes, apart from the impulses of patriotism and public spirit, had not much to do in turning him towards a course of life so little indicated by anything in its beginning. There is no appearance that Sheridan cared very much for literary fame. His taste was not refined nor his mind highly cultivated; he thought, like Byron and George III., that Shakspeare was a much over-rated writer. He was very difficult to please in his own diction, and elaborated both written dialogues and spoken speeches with the most anxious care; but fame as an author was not what he looked for or cared for, nor would such a reputation have answered his purpose. Social success was what he aimed at—he wanted to be among the first, not in intellect, but in fact : to win his way into the highest elevation, and to stand there on an equality with whosoever should approach. For such an aim as this, literature, unaided, can do but little. The days of patronage, in which an author was the natural hanger-on and dependent of a great man, are not so dissimilar as they appear, to our own : except in so far that the patron in former days paid a more just equivalent for the distinction which his famous hanger-on might give him. In modern times the poet who is content to swell the train of a great family and get himself into society by that means, gets a very precarious footing in the enchanted circle, and is never recognised as one of the fine people who give him a great deal of vague praise but nothing else. This was a sort of favour which Sheridan would never have brooked. He had made that clear from the beginning. He would not creep into favour or wait for invitations to great houses, but boldly and at once took the initiative, and himself invited the great world, and became the host and entertainer of persons infinitely more important than himself. There is no subject on which the easy morality of society has

been more eloquent than on the folly of the artist and
man of letters who, not content with having all houses
thrown open to them, insist upon entertaining in their
own persons, and providing for dukes and princes what
can be but a feeble imitation, at the best, of their own
lordly fare.   But we think that the sympathetic reader,
when he looks into it, will find many inducements to a
charitable interpretation of such seeming extravagance.
The artist is received everywhere : he is among, but not
of, the most brilliant assemblages, perhaps even he lends
them part of their attractions : but even in the very
stare with which the fine ladies and fine gentlemen
contemplate him, he will read the certainty that he is a
spectacle, a thing to be looked at—but not one of them.
In his own house the balance is redressed, and he holds
his fit place.   Something of this feeling perhaps was in
the largeness of hospitality with which Sir Walter Scott
threw open his doors, a magnanimous yet half-disdainful
generosity, as who should say, "If you will stare, come
here and do it, where I am your superior as master of
my house, your inferior only out of high courtesy and
honour to my guest."   Sheridan was not like Scott ; but
he was a proud man.   And it pleased his sense of humour
that the Duchess of Devonshire, still balancing in her
mind whether she should receive these young people,
should be his guest instead, and have the grace extended
to her, instead of first extending it to him.   And no
doubt his determination to acquire for himself, if by any
possibility he could, a position in which he should be on
the same level as the greatest,—not admitted on suffer-
ance but an indispensable part of society,—had something to do with the earnestness with which he threw

himself into public life. The origin of a great statesman is unimportant. Power is a dazzling cloak which covers every imperfection, whereas fame of other kinds but emphasizes and points them out.

This is by no means to say that Sheridan had no higher meaning in his political life. He was very faithful to his party and to Fox, and later to the less respectable patron with whom his name is associated, with little reward of any kind. But he was not an enthusiast like Burke, any more than a philosopher, nor was his patriotism or his character worthy to be named along with those of that noble and unfortunate politician, with whom for one period of their lives Sheridan was brought into a sort of rivalship. Burke was at all times a leading and originating spirit, penetrating the surface of things; Sheridan a light-hearted adventurer in politics as well as in life, with keen perceptions and a brilliant way of now and then hitting out a right suggestion and finding often a fine and effective thing to say. It is impossible, however, to think of him as influencing public opinion in any great or lasting way. He acted on the great stage of public life, on a large scale, the part of the Horatios—nay, let us say the Mercutios of the theatre,—sometimes by stress of circumstances coming to the front with a noble piece of rhetoric or even of pure poetry to deliver once in a way, always giving a brilliancy of fine costume and dazzle and glitter on the second level. If the motives which led him to that greatest of arenas were not solely the ardours of patriotism, they were not the meaner stimulants of self-interest. He had no thought of making his fortune out of his country; if he hoped to get advancement by her, and honour, and

a place among the highest, these desires were at least
not mercenary, and might with very little difficulty be
translated into that which is still considered a lofty
weakness—that which Milton calls the last infirmity of
noble minds—a desire for fame.   It is easy to make
this pursuit look very fine and dazzling: it may be
mean enough on the other hand.

It was in 1780, when he was twenty-nine, that
Sheridan entered Parliament.   It was his pride that he
was not brought in for any pocket borough, but was
elected by the town of Stafford, in which the freemen of
the burgh had the privilege of choosing their member.
How they exercised that choice—agreeably, no doubt, to
themselves, and very much so to the candidate, whose
path was thus extraordinarily simplified—may be seen
in the account of Sheridan's election expenses, where
there is one such broad and simple entry as the following :
—"248 *Burgesses, paid* £5 5s. *each."*   A petition against his
return and that of his colleague was not unnaturally presented, but came to nothing, and Sheridan's first speech
was made in his own defence.   It was not a very successful one.   The House, attracted by his reputation in
other scenes, and by the name, which by this time was
so well known in society, heard him "with particular
attention;" but he, whose future appearances were to
carry with them the enthusiastic applauses of the most
difficult audience in England, had to submit to the force
of ridicule, which he himself so often and so brilliantly
applied in after times, and to that still more appalling
ordeal, the chill attention and disappointment of his
hearers.   He is said to have rushed up to the reporters'
gallery where Woodfall was busy with his notes, and to

have asked his opinion. "I am sorry to say I do not think this is your line," said that candid friend; "you had much better have stuck to your former pursuits," on hearing which Sheridan rested his head on his hands for a few minutes and then vehemently exclaimed—"It is in me, however, and, by G——, it shall come out." The quiver of disappointment, excitement, and determination in this outcry is very characteristic. It did come out, and that at no very great interval, as everybody knows.

Sheridan entered political life at a time when it was full of commotion and conflict. The American war was in full progress, kept up by the obstinacy of the King and the subserviency of his Ministers against almost all the better feeling of England, and in face of a steadily increasing opposition, which extended from statesmen like Burke and Fox down to the other extremity of society — to the Surrey peasant who was William Cobbett's father, and who "would not have suffered his best friend to drink success to the King's arms." Politics were exceptionally keen and bitter, since they were in a great measure a personal conflict between a small number of men pitted against each other—men of the same training, position, and traditions, but split into two hereditary factions, and contending fiercely for the mastery—while the nation had little more to do with it than to stand at a distance vaguely looking on, with no power of action and even an imperfect knowledge of the proceedings of Parliament, which was supposed to represent and certainly did rule them. That the public had any right at all to a knowledge of what was going on in the debates of the two Houses, was but a recent idea,

and still the reports were to the highest degree meagre
and unsatisfactory; while the expression of public feeling through the newspapers was still in a very early
stage. But within the narrow circle which held power,
and which also held the potential criticism which is the
soul of party in England, the differences of opinion were
heightened by personal emulations, and violent opposi-
tions existed between men of whom we find a difficulty
in discovering now why it was that they did not work con-
tinuously side by side, instead of, with spasmodic changes,
in separate parties. There were points, especially in
respect to the representation of the people, in which Pitt
was more liberal than Fox: and the Whigs, thenceforward
to be associated with every project of electoral reform,
were Conservative to the highest degree in this respect,
and defended their close boroughs with all the zeal of
proprietorship. In 1780, when Sheridan entered Parliament, the King took an active part in every act of the
Government, with an obedient minister under his orders,
and a Parliament filled with dependents and pensioners.
No appeal to the country was possible in those days, or
even thought of. No appeal, indeed, was possible anywhere. It was the final battle-ground, where every com-
batant had his antagonist, and the air was always loud
with cries of battle. The Whig party had it very much
at heart to reduce the power of the Court, and clear out
the accumulated corruptions which stifled wholesome life
in the House of Commons; but they had no very strong
desire to widen the franchise or admit the mass of the
people to political privileges. Sheridan, indeed, had taken
part along with Fox during that very year in a Reform
meeting which had passed certain " Resolutions on the

state of the representation," advocating the right of the
people to universal suffrage and annual parliaments; but
it is scarcely possible to believe that their share in it was
more than a pleasantry. "Always say that you are for
annual parliaments and universal suffrage, then you
are safe," Fox is reported to have said, with no doubt
a twinkle in his eye: while Burke made merry over the
still more advanced opinions of some visionary politicians,
"who—founding on the latter words of a statute of
Edward III. that a parliament should be holden every
year once, and more often if need be—were known by the
denomination of Oftener-if-need-bes." "For my part,"
he would add, "I am an Oftener-if-need-be." Thus the
statesmen jested at their ease, very sure that nothing
would come of it, and not unwilling to amuse themselves with schemes so extravagant.

Among the leaders of the party with which Sheridan
threw in his fortunes, a very high, perhaps the highest
place was held by Burke, who was in some respects like
himself, a man of humble origin, with none of the dignified antecedents possessed by the others, though with a
genius superior to them all, and the highest oratorical
powers: the countryman, perhaps the model, perhaps
the rival, of the new recruit with whom he had so many
external points of likeness. It is curious to find two
such men, both Irishmen, both in the higher sense of
the word adventurers, with the same command of eloquence, at the head of a great English political party at
the same moment. There does not seem ever to have
been the same cordiality of friendship between them,
notwithstanding, or perhaps in consequence of, the similarity of their circumstances, as existed between each of

them and the genial and gracious Fox, whose lovableness
and sweetness of nature seem to have vanquished every
heart and kept an atmosphere of pleasantness about
him, which breathes through every page in which he is
named. To have come at once into the close companion-
ship of such men as these, to be permitted to share
their counsels, to add his word to theirs, to unite with
them in all their undertakings, and, dearest joy of all, to
fight by their side in every parliamentary tumult, and
defy the Tories and the Fates along with them, was an
elevation which might well have turned the head of the
young dramatist who had so little right to expect any
such astonishing advancement.

And the firmament all around this keen and eager
centre was gloomy and threatening;—in America the
war advancing to that stage in which continuance becomes
an impossibility and a climax of one kind or another
must be arrived at ;—in Ireland, which in those days was
the Ireland of the Protestant ascendency, the reverse of
everything that calls itself Irish now—a sort of chronic
semi-rebellion.   In India, where the Company were
making their conquests and forming their government
in independence of any direct imperial control, a hundred
questions arising which would have to be settled ere long ;
—in France, the gathering of the revolutionary storm,
which was soon to burst and affect all the world.   A
more exciting outlook could not be.   The existing generation did not perhaps realise the crowding in of troubles
from every side as we do, to whom the whole panorama
is rolled out ; while naturally there were matters which
we take very calmly as knowing them to have passed
quite innocuously over the great vitality of England,

which to them looked dangers unspeakable. But we
need not attempt to enter here into that detailed narrative of the political life of the period which would be
necessary did we trace Sheridan through every debate
he took part in, and every political movement in which
he was engaged. This has been recently done in a former
volume of this series with a completeness and care which
would render a repeated effort of the same character a
superfluity, even were the writer bold enough to venture
upon such a competition. The political surroundings
and events of Burke's public life were to a great extent
those of Sheridan also, and it would be almost an imper-
tinence to retrace the ground which Mr. Morley has
gone over so thoroughly. We will therefore confine
ourselves to an indication of the chief movements in
which Sheridan was personally involved, and in which
his impetuous eloquence produced an effect which has
made his name historical. This result was not immediately attained; but it is evident that the leaders of the
party must have very soon perceived how valuable a
recruit the young member for Stafford was, since he was
carried with them into office after little more than two
years of parliamentary life, in the short accession to
power of the Whig party after the fall of Lord North.
What he had done to merit this speedy elevation it is
difficult to see. He was made one of the under-secretaries
of state in the Rockingham ministry, and had to all appearance the ball at his foot. The feeling entertained on this
subject by his family, watching from across the Channel
with much agitation of hope the extraordinary and unaccountable advance he was making, is admirably set
forth in the following letter from his brother :—

"I am much obliged to you for your early intelligence concerning the fate of the ministry, and give you joy on the occasion, notwithstanding your sorrow for the departure of the good opposition. I understand very well what you mean by this sorrow ; but as you may be now in a situation in which you may obtain some substantial advantage to yourself, for God's sake improve the opportunity to the utmost, and don't let dreams of empty fame (of which you have had enough in conscience) carry you away from your solid interests. I return you many thanks for Fox's letter ; I mean for your intention to make him write one—for as your good intentions always satisfy your conscience, and that you seem to think the carrying of them into execution to be a mere trifling ceremony, as well omitted as not, your friends must always take the will for the deed. I will forgive you, however, on condition that you will for once in your life consider that though the will alone may perfectly satisfy yourself, your friends would be a little more gratified if they were sometimes to see it accompanied by the deed—and let me be the first upon whom you try the experiment. If the people here are not to share the fate of their patrons, but are suffered to continue in the government of this country, I believe you will have it in your power, as I am certain it will be in your inclination, to fortify my claims upon them, by recommendation from your side of the water, in such a manner as to insure to me what I have a right to expect from them, but of which I can have no certainty without that assistance. I wish the present people may continue here, because I certainly have claims upon them, and considering the footing that Lord C—— and Charles Fox are on, a recommendation from the latter would now have every weight ; it would be drawing a bill upon Government here, payable at sight, which they dare not protest. So, dear Dick, I shall rely upon you that this will *really* be done ; and, to confess the truth, unless it be done and speedily, I shall be completely ruined."

The delightful *naïveté* of this letter, and its half-provoked tone of good advice and superior wisdom, throws a humorous gleam over the situation. That it was

Sheridan's bounden duty "for God's sake" to take care
that no foolish ideas should prevent him from securing
substantial advantage to himself, and in the meantime and
at once an appointment for his brother, is too far beyond
question to be discussed; but the writer cannot but feel
an impatient conviction that Dick is quite capable of
neglecting both for some flummery about fame, which is
really almost too much to be put up with.   Charles Sheridan got his appointment, which was that of Secretary
of War in Ireland, a post which he enjoyed for many years.
But the "substantial advantage" which he considered it
his brother's duty to secure for himself never came.

Sheridan's first taste of the sweets of office was a very
short one.   The Rockingham ministry remained in but
four months, during which time they succeeded in
clearing away a considerable portion of the accumulated uncleanness which had recently neutralised the
power of the House of Commons.   The measures passed
in this brief period dealt a fatal blow at that overwhelming influence of the Crown which had brought about so
many disasters, and, by a stern cutting off of the means
of corruption, "mark the date when the direct bribery of
members absolutely ceased," which is the highest praise.
But Lord Rockingham died and Lord Shelburne succeeded him, who represented but one side of the party,
and the withdrawal of Fox from the ministry brought
Sheridan back—it is said partly against his own judgment, which says all the more for his fidelity to his
leader—into the irresponsibility and unprofitableness of
opposition.   The famous Coalition, which came into being
a year later, restored him to office as Secretary of the
Treasury.   Sheridan went on forming his style as a politi-

cal speaker with great care and perseverance through all
these vicissitudes. At first he is said to have written his
speeches out carefully, and even learnt them by heart,
"using for this purpose," Moore tells us, "the same sort
of copy-books which he had employed in the first rough
draughts of his plays." Afterwards a scribble on a piece
of paper was enough to guide him, and sometimes it is
very evident he made a telling retort or a bold attack
without preparation at all. One of these, preserved in the
collection of his speeches, has a vivid gleam of restrained
excitement and personal feeling in it which gives it an
interest more human than political. It occurred in
the discussion by the House of the preliminaries of
the treaty afterwards known as the Treaty of Ver-
sailles, in which the independence of America was formally recognised. In Sheridan's speech on the subject
he had referred pointedly to Pitt, who had become
Chancellor of the Exchequer in Lord Shelburne's administration, and who had objected to something in a
previous debate as inconsistent with the established
usage of the House. "This convinced him," Sheridan
said, "that the right honourable gentleman was more a
practical politician than an experienced one," and that
"his years and his very early political exaltation had
not permitted him to look whether there had been pre-
cedents, or to acquire a knowledge of the journals of the
House." Pitt resented this assault upon his youth as
every young man is apt to do, and did his best to turn
the war into the enemy's camp. Here is the somewhat
ungenerous assault he made, one, however, which has
been repeated almost as often as there have been eminent
literary men in public life :—

"No man admired more than he did the abilities of that right honourable gentleman, the elegant sallies of his thought, the gay effusions of his fancy, his dramatic turns, and his epigrammatic points ; and if they were reserved for a proper stage, they would no doubt receive what the honourable gentleman's abilities always did receive, the plaudits of the audience ; and it would be his fortune '*sin plausu gaudere theatri*.' But this was not the proper scene for the exhibition of these elegancies ; and he therefore must beg leave to call the attention of the house to the serious consideration of the very important questions now before them."

This unhandsome reference to Sheridan's theatrical fame was one of those uncalled-for and unworthy attacks which give the person assailed an enormous advantage over the assailant ; and Sheridan was quite equal to the occasion.

"Mr. Sheridan then rose to an explanation, which being made, he took notice of that particular sort of personality which the right honourable gentleman had thought proper to introduce. He need not comment upon it—the propriety, the taste, the gentlemanly point of it, must have been obvious to the House. But, said Mr. Sheridan, let me assure the right honourable gentleman that I do now, and will at any time when he chooses to repeat this sort of allusion, meet it with the most sincere good humour. Nay, I will say more, flattered and encouraged by the right honourable gentleman's panegyric on my talents, if I ever again engage in the compositions he alludes to, I may be tempted to an act of presumption—to attempt an improvement on one of Ben Jonson's best characters—the character of the Angry Boy in the *Alchymist*."[1]

Apart from sparrings of this description, however, in which his light hand and touch were always effective,

[1] This threat was carried out by the issue of a pretended playbill, in which not only was the part of the Angry Boy allotted to Pitt, but the audacious wit proceeded to assign that of Surly to "His ——"!

Sheridan gradually proceeded to take a larger part in the
business of the House, his speeches being full of energy,
lucidity, and point, as well as of unfailing humour. But
it was not till the celebrated impeachment of Warren
Hastings, one of the most dramatic episodes in parliamentary history, that he rose to the fulness of his
eloquence and power. The story of that episode has
been often told : almost more often and more fully than
any other chapter of modern history : and everybody
knows how and why it was that—having added to the
wealth of his chiefs and the power of the nation, and
with a consciousness in his mind of having done much
to open up and confirm an immense new empire to his
country—this Indian ruler and lawgiver, astonished,
found himself confronted by the indignation of all that
was best and greatest in England, and ere he knew
was placed at the bar to account for what he had
done, the treasures he had exacted, and the oppressions
with which he had crushed the native states and their
rulers.

> " Is India free ? and does she wear her plumed
> And jewelled turban with a smile of peace ?
> Or do we grind her still ?"

Cowper had said as he opened his scanty newspaper in the
fireside quiet at Olney some time before. The manner
in which such a prize was added to the British crown
has slipped from the general memory nowadays, and
we are apt to forget how many deeds were done on
that argument that would not bear the light of public
inquiry. But this great trial will always stand as a proof
that the time had arrived in the history of England

when she would no longer tolerate the highhanded proceedings of the conqueror, and that even national aggrand-
isement was not a strong enough inducement to make
her overlook injustice and cruelty though in the ends of
the earth.

It was Burke who originated the idea of impeachment
for Warren Hastings : it was Pitt, by his unexpected
vote with the accusing party, who made it practicable;
but Sheridan was the hero of the occasion.   One of the
worst charges against Hastings was his conduct to the
princesses of Oude, the old and helpless Begums whom he
imprisoned and ill used in order to draw from them their
treasures ; and this moving subject, the one of all others
best adapted for him, it was given to Sheridan to set
forth in all the atrocity of its circumstances, and with all
the power of eloquent indignation of which he was
master, before the House, as one of the grounds for the
impeachment.   The speech was ill reported, and has not
been preserved in a form which does it justice, but we
have such details of its effect as have rarely been laid up
in history.   The following account, corroborated by
many witnesses, is taken from the summary given at the
head of the extracts from this oration in the collection
of Sheridan's speeches :—

" For five hours and a half Mr. Sheridan commanded the
universal interest and admiration of the house (which from
the expectation of the day was uncommonly crowded) by an
oration of almost unexampled excellence, uniting the most
convincing closeness and accuracy of argument with the most
luminous precision and perspicuity of language, and alter-
nately giving form and energy to truth by solid and substantial
reasoning ; and enlightening the most extensive and involved
subjects with the purest clearness of logic and the brightest

splendours of rhetoric. Every prejudice, every prepossession, was gradually overcome by the force of this extraordinary combination of keen but liberal discrimination ; of brilliant yet argumentative wit. So fascinated were the auditors by his eloquence that when Mr. Sheridan sat down the whole house —the members, peers, and strangers—involuntarily joined in a tumult of applause, and adopted a mode of expressing their admiration, new and irregular in the house, by loudly and repeatedly clapping with their hands. Mr. Burke declared it to be the most astonishing effort of eloquence, argument, and wit united of which there was any record or tradition. Mr. Fox said, ' All that he had ever heard—all that he had ever read—when compared with it dwindled into nothing, and vanished like vapour before the sun.' Mr. Pitt acknowledged that it surpassed all the eloquence of ancient or of modern times, and possessed everything that genius or art could furnish to agitate and control the human mind. The effects it produced were proportioned to its merits. After a considerable suspension of the debate, one of the friends of Mr. Hastings—Mr. Burgess—with some difficulty obtained for a short time a hearing ; but, finding the house too strongly affected by what they had heard to listen to him with favour, sat down again. Several members confessed they had come down strongly prepossessed in favour of the person accused, and imagined nothing less than a miracle could have wrought so entire a revolution in their sentiments. Others declared that though they could not resist the conviction that flashed upon their minds, yet they wished to have leave to cool before they were called upon to vote ; and though they were persuaded it would require another miracle to produce another change in their opinions, yet for the sake of decorum they thought it proper that the debate should be adjourned. Mr. Fox and Mr. A. Taylor strongly opposed this proposition, contending that it was not less absurd than unparliamentary to defer coming to a vote for no other reason that had been alleged than because members were too firmly convinced ; but Mr. Pitt concurring with the opinions of the former, the debate was adjourned."

What Pitt said was that they were all still " under

the wand of the enchanter;" while other members individually made similar acknowledgments. "Sir William Dalton immediately moved an adjournment, confessing that in the state of mind in which Mr. Sheridan's speech had left him it was impossible for him to give a determinate opinion." That great audience, the most difficult, the most important in Christendom, was overwhelmed like a company of sympathetic women, by the quick communicating thrill of intellectual excitement, of generous ardour, of wonder, terror, pity. It was like a fine intoxication which nobody could resist. Here is another amusing instance of the influence it exercised :—

"The late Mr. Logan . . . author of a most masterly defence of Mr. Hastings, went that day to the House of Commons prepossessed for the accused, and against the accuser. At the expiration of the first hour he said to a friend, 'All this is declamatory assertion without proof ;' when the second was finished, 'This is a most wonderful oration.' At the close of the third, 'Mr. Hastings has acted most unjustifiably ;' the fourth, 'Mr. Hastings is a most atrocious criminal ;' and at last, 'Of all monsters of iniquity, the most enormous is Warren Hastings !'"

It was no wonder if the astonished members, with a feeling that this transformation was a kind of magic, unaccountable by any ordinary rule, were afraid of themselves, and dared not venture on any practical step until they had cooled down a little. It is the most remarkable instance on record in modern times of the amazing power of oratory. The public interest had flagged in the matter, notwithstanding the vehement addresses of Burke, but it awoke with a leap of excitement at this magic touch ; and when, some months later, the trial took place according to an old and long-disused

formula in Westminster Hall, the whole world flocked to
listen. Macaulay has painted the scene for us in one of
his most picturesque pages. The noble hall full of noble
people; the peers in their ermine; the judges in their
red robes; the grey old walls hung with scarlet; the
wonderful audience in the galleries; the Queen herself
with all her ladies, among them the lively, weary little
frizzled head with so much in it, of Fanny Burney, pre-
judiced yet impressionable, looking over Her Majesty's
shoulder, and such faces as those of the lovely Duchess
of Devonshire, the haughty beauty of Mrs. Fitzherbert,
the half-angelic sweetness of Sheridan's wife, with many
another less known to fame, and all the men whose
names confer a glory on their age. "In the midst of
the blaze of red draperies an open space had been fitted
up with green benches and tables for the Commons."
The great commoners who conducted the prosecution,
the managers of the impeachment as they were called,
appeared in full dress, even Fox, the negligent, "paying
the illustrious tribunal the compliment of wearing a
bag and sword." Amidst these public prosecutors the
two kindred forms of Burke and Sheridan, both with a
certain bluntness of feature which indicated their
race, the latter at least, with those brilliant eyes
which are so often the mark of genius, were the principal figures.

This wonderful scene lasted for months : and it
may be supposed what an exciting entertainment was
thus provided for society, ever anxious for a new
sensation. Burke spoke for four days, and with great
effect. But it was when it came to the turn of
Sheridan to repeat his wonderful effort, and once more

plead the cause of the robbed and insulted Princesses,
that public excitement rose to its height. "The curiosity of the public to hear him was unbounded. His
sparkling and highly finished declamation lasted two
days : but the hall was crowded to suffocation the whole
time. It was said that fifty guineas had been paid for a
single ticket." His speech, as a matter of fact, extended
over four days, and the trial, which had begun in
February, had lasted out till June, dragging its slow
length along, when it came to this climax. Many of
his colleagues considered this speech greatly inferior
to the first outburst of eloquence on the same subject
with which he had electrified the House of Commons.
"Sheridan's speech on the Begums in the House admirable ; in Westminster Hall contemptible," Lord Granville
said, and such was also the opinion of Fox. But a
greater than either was of a different opinion. In the
sitting of the House held on the 6th of June, after an
exciting morning spent in Westminster Hall, a certain
Mr. Burgess, the same pertinacious person who had risen
to speak in favour of Hastings, while still St. Stephens
was resounding with applause and inarticulate with emotion on the day of Sheridan's first speech, got up once
more, while all minds were again occupied by the same
subject, to call the attention of the House to some small
matter of finance. He was transfixed immediately by
the spear of Burke. "He could not avoid offering his
warmest congratulations to the honourable gentleman
on his having chosen that glorious day, after the triumph
of the morning, to bring forward a business of such an
important nature," cried the great orator with contemptuous sarcasm ; and he went on to applaud the

powerful mind of the stolid partisan who had proved himself capable of such an effort, "after every other member had been struck dumb with astonishment and admiration at the wonderful eloquence of his friend Mr. Sheridan, who had that day again surprised the thousands who hung with rapture on his accents, by such a display of talents as was unparalleled in the annals of oratory, and so did the highest honour to himself, to that House, and to the country."

The reader will be perhaps more interested, in this deluge of applause, to hear how the wife, of whom perhaps Sheridan was not worthy, yet who was not herself without blame, a susceptible creature, with a fine nature always showing under the levities and excitements that circumstances had made natural to her, exulted in his triumph.

"I have delayed writing (the letter is to her sister-in-law) till I could gratify myself and you by sending you the news of our dear Dick's triumph,—of our triumph I may call it,— for surely no one in the slightest degree connected with him but must feel proud and happy. It is impossible, my dear woman, to convey to you the delight, the astonishment, the adoration, he has excited in the breasts of every class of people. Every party prejudice has been overcome by a display of genius, eloquence, and goodness, which no one with anything like a heart about them could have listened to without being the wiser and the better all the rest of their lives. What must *my* feelings be, you only can imagine. To tell you the truth, it is with some difficulty that I can ' let down my mind,' as Mr. Burke said afterwards, to talk or think on that or any other subject. But pleasure too exquisite becomes pain, and I am at this moment suffering from the delightful anxieties of last week."

This triumph, however, like Sheridan's previous successes, would seem to have been won by a fit of accidental exertion; for it was still as difficult as ever to keep him in harness and secure his attention. A letter quoted in Moore's life from Burke to Mrs. Sheridan makes the difficulty very apparent. The great statesman begins by skilful praise of Sheridan's abilities to propitiate his wife: and then implores Mrs. Sheridan's aid in "prevailing upon Mr. Sheridan to be with us this day at half after three in the Committee." The paymaster of Oude was to be examined, he adds with anxious emphasis. "Oude is Mr. Sheridan's particular province; and I do most seriously ask that he would favour us with his assistance." This proves how little he was to be relied upon, even now, in the very moment of triumph. Yet on the very next page we read of the elaborate manner in which his speech was prepared and of the exertions of his domestic helpers in arranging and classifying his materials; and he seems from Moore's account to have laboured indefatigably to acquire the necessary knowledge.

" There is a large pamphlet of Mr. Hastings," Moore tells us, " consisting of more than two hundred pages, copied out mostly in her (Mrs. Sheridan's) writing, with some assistance from another female hand.   The industry, indeed, of all about him was called into requisition for the great occasion : some busy with the pen and scissors making extracts, some pasting and stitching his scattered memorandums in their places, so that there was scarcely a member of his family that could not boast of having contributed his share to the mechanical construction of this speech.   The pride of its success was of course equally participated : and Edwards, a favourite servant of Mr. Sheridan, was long celebrated for his professed imitation of the manner in which his master delivered (what seems to have struck Edwards as the finest part of the speech) his closing words, ' My Lords, I have done.' "

Macaulay informs us that Sheridan "contrived with a knowledge of stage effect, which his father might have envied, to sink back as if exhausted into the arms of Burke, who hugged him with the energy of generous admiration" when the speech was done.

In every way this was the highest point of Sheridan's career. Engaged in the greatest work to which civilised man can turn his best faculties, the government of his country, either potentially or by criticism, censure, and the restraining power of opposition, he had made his way without previous training, or any adventitious circumstances in his favour, to the very front rank of statesmen. When wrong was to be chastised and right established, he was one of the foremost in the work. His party did nothing without him : his irregular ways, the difficulty which there was even in getting him to attend a meeting, were all overlooked. Rather would the Whig leaders invent, like the proprietors of the theatre in former days, a snare in which to take him, or plead with his wife for her assistance, than do without Sheridan. This was what the player's son, the dramatist and stage manager, who was nobody, without education, without fortune, had come to. He was thirty-seven when he stood upon this apex of applause and honour — *al mezzo di cammin di nostra vita.* Had he died then, the wonder of his fame and greatness would have been lessened by no painful drawback. If he were extravagant, reckless, given to the easier vices, so were other men of his generation—and pecuniary embarrassment only becomes appalling when it reaches the stage of actual want, and when squalor and misery follow in its train. We linger upon the picture of

these triumphs—triumphs as legitimate, as noble, and
worthy as ever man won—in which if perhaps there
was no such enthusiasm of generous sentiment as moved
Burke, there was at least the sincere movement of a
more volatile nature against cruelty and injustice. It
does not in reality enhance the greatness of a mental
effort that it is made in the cause of humanity—but it
enormously increases its weight and influence with mankind. And it was an extraordinary piece of good fortune
for Sheridan, in a career made up hitherto of happy hits
and splendid pieces of luck, that he should happily have
lighted upon a subject for his greatest effort, which
should not only afford scope for all his gifts, his impul-
sive generosity and tenderheartedness, as well, we may
add, as that tendency to claptrap and inflated diction
which is almost always successful with the multitude,—
but at the same time should secure for himself as the
magnanimous advocate a large share in that sympathy
of the audience for the helpless and injured, which his
eloquence raised into temporary passion. His subject,
his oratorical power, the real enthusiasm which inspired
him, even if that enthusiasm took fire at its own flame,
and was more on account of Brinsley Sheridan than
of the Begums, all helped in the magical effect. Even
poor Mrs. Sheridan, who knew better than any one
wherein the orator was defective, exulted in his triumph
as "a display of genius, and eloquence, *and goodness.*"
He was the champion of humanity, the defender of the
weak and helpless. No doubt, in the glow of interest
in his own subject to which he had worked himself
up, he felt all this more fervently even than his audience,
which again added infinitely to his power.

The trial came to nothing, as everybody knows. It lingered over years of tedious discussion, and through worlds of wearisome verbiage, and only got decided in 1795, when the accused, whose sins by this time had been half forgotten, whose foolish plans for himself were altogether out of mind, and whose good qualities had come round again to the recollection of the world, was acquitted. By that time the breaking up of the party which had brought him to the bar, so touchingly described by Macaulay, had come to pass; and though Sheridan still held by Fox, Burke had fallen apart from them both for ever. Professor Smyth, in his valuable little *Memoir of Sheridan*, gives a description of the orator's preparation for the postscriptal speech which he had to deliver six years after in 1794, in answer to the pleas of Hastings' counsel, which is very characteristic. Sheridan arrived suddenly one evening at the country residence where his son Tom was staying with Smyth the tutor— with his chaise full of papers, and announced his intention of getting through them all, and being ready with his reply the day after to-morrow. "The day after to-morrow! this day six months you mean," cried Smyth in consternation. Altogether Sheridan would seem to have taken five or six days to this trying work, recalling the recollection of his highest triumph, and refreshing his memory as to the facts, after a long and sad interval, filled with many misfortunes and down-falls.—He never stirred "out of his room for three days and evenings, and each of the three nights, till the motes, he told me, were coming into his eyes, though the strongest and finest that ever man was blest with," Smyth informs us. He dined every day with the tutor and Tom, the

bright and delightful boy who was a sweeter and more
innocent reproduction of himself—and during these meals
Smyth found that it was his part to listen, "making a
slight occasional comment on what he told me he had
been doing."

"On the morning appointed he went off early in a chaise
and four to Grosvenor Street, and none of us, Tom told me,
were to come near him till the speech was over. When he
came into the manager's box he was in full dress, and his
countenance had assumed an ashen colour that I had never
before observed. No doubt Cicero himself must have quailed
before so immense and magnificent an audience as was now
assembled to hear him. He was evidently tried to the utmost,
every nerve and faculty within him put into complete requisition."

No doubt Sheridan felt the ghost of his own glory
rising up as a rival to him in this renewed and so
changed appearance. The tutor felt that "his aspect
was that of a perfect orator, and thought he was listening to some being of a totally different nature from himself:" but this postscriptal harangue has had no record
of fame. And already the leaf was turned over, the
dark side of life come upward, and Sheridan's glory on
the wane.

CHAPTER V.

MIDDLE AGE.

THE middle of life is the testing-ground of character and strength. There are many who hold a foremost place in the heat of youth, but sink behind when that first energy is played out; and there are many whose follies happily die, and whose true strength is only known when serious existence with its weights and responsibilities comes upon them. Many are the revelations of this sober age. Sins which were but venial in the boy grow fatal in the man. The easy indolence, the careless good fellowship, the rollicking humour which we laugh at while we condemn them in youth, become coarser, vulgarer, meaner in maturity, and acquire a character of selfishness and brutality which was not theirs in the time of hope. In Sheridan's age, above all others, the sins of a Charles Surface were easily pardoned to a young man. He was better liked for being something of a rake; his prodigality and neglect of all prudent precautions, his rashness in every enterprise, his headlong career, which it was always believed something might turn up to guide into a better development at the end, were proofs of the generosity and truth of a character concealing nothing. All this was natural at five-and-twenty. But at thirty-five, and still more at forty, the world gets weary of Charles Surface. His lightheartedness becomes want of feeling,—his rashness unmanly folly,—his shortcomings are everywhere judged by a different standard; and the middle-aged man whom neither regard for his honour, his duty, nor his family, can curb and restrain, who takes his own way whoever suffers, and is continually playing at the highest stakes for mere life, is deserted by public opinion, and can be defended by his friends with only faltering excuses. Sheridan had been such a man in his youth. He had dared everything, and won much from fate. Without a penny to begin with, or any of that capital of industry, perseverance, and determination which serves instead of money, he got possession of and enjoyed all the luxuries of wealth. He did more than this; he became one of the leading names in England, foremost on imperial occasions, and known wherever news of England was prized or read; and through all his earlier years the world had laughed at his shifts, his hairbreadth escapes, the careless prodigality of nature, which made it certain that by a sudden and violent effort at the end he could always make up for all deficiencies. It was a jest that

> " Of wit, of taste, of fancy, we'll debate,
> If Sheridan for once be not too late."

And in the artificial world of the theatre, the recklessness of the man and all his eccentricities had something in them which suited that abode of strong contrasts and effects. But after a course of years the world began to get tired of always waiting for Sheridan, always finding that he had forgotten his word and his appointments, and never read, much less answered, his letters. There came a moment when everybody with one accord ceased and even refused to be amused by these eccentricities any longer, and found them to be stale jests, insolences, and characterised by a selfish disregard of everybody's comfort but his own.

This natural protest no doubt was accompanied by a gradual development of all that was most insupportable in Sheridan's nature. The entire absence in him of the faculty of self-control grew with his advancing years ; but it was not till Providence had interposed and deprived him of the wife who, in her sweet imperfection, had yet done much for him, that any serious change happened in his fortunes. He lost his father in 1788, very shortly after his great triumph. There is no very evident sign that Thomas Sheridan ever changed his mind in respect to his sons, or ceased to prefer the prim and prudent Charles, who had bidden his brother not to be so foolishly moved by thoughts of fame as to neglect the substantial advantages which office might ensure to him. But it was Richard who attended upon the old man's deathbed, moved with an almost excessive filial devotion and regret, and buried him, and intended to place a fine inscription over him, written by no hand but that of Dr. Parr, the best of scholars. It was never done : but Charles Sheridan (who was present, however, neither at the sickbed nor the grave) had already intimated the conviction of the family that in Dick's case the will had to be taken for the deed. This loss, however, was little to the greater blow which he suffered a few years later. Mrs. Sheridan is one of those characters who, without doing anything to make themselves remarkable, yet leave a certain fragrance behind them as of something fine, and tender, and delicate. The reader will remember the letter referred to in the first chapter, in which she recounts her early troubles to her sympathising friend, a pretty and sentimental composition, with a touch of Evelina (who was the young lady's contemporary) in its confidences, and still more of Lydia Languish, whose prototype she might well have been. And there is a certain reflection of Lydia Languish throughout her life, softened by the cessation of sentimental dilemmas, but never without a turn for the romantic. That she was a good wife to Sheridan there seems little doubt: the accounts of the theatre kept in her handwriting, the long and careful extracts made and information prepared by her to help him—even the appeals to her on every side, from her father, anxious about the theatre and its business, up to Mr. Burke in the larger political sphere, all confident that she would be able to do what nobody else could do, keep Sheridan to an appointment—show what her office was between him and the world. Within doors, of all characters for the reckless wit to enact, he was the Falkland of his own drama, maddening a more hapless Julia, driving her a hundred times out of patience and out of heart with innumerable suspicions, jealousies, harassments of every kind. And no man who lived the life he was living, with the most riotous company of the time, could be a very good husband. He left her to go into society alone, in all her beauty and charm,—the St. Cecilia of many worshippers,—still elegant, lovely, and sentimental, an involuntary siren, accustomed to homage, and perhaps liking it a little, as

most people, even the wisest, do. There could be no
want of tenderness to her husband in the woman who
wrote the letter of happy pride and adoration quoted in
the last chapter ; and yet she was not herself untouched
by scandal, and it was whispered that a young, handsome, romantic Irishman, in all the glory of national
enthusiasm and with the shadow of tragedy already
upon him, had moved her heart. It is not necessary to
enter into any such vague and shadowy tale. No permanent alienation appears to have ever arisen between
her and her husband, though there were many painful
scenes, consequent upon the too finely-strung nerves,
which is often another name for irritability and impatience, of both. Sheridan's sister, who lived in his house
for a short time after her father's death, gives us a most
charming picture of this sweet and attractive woman.

"I have been here almost a week in perfect quiet. While
there was company in the house I stayed in my room, and
since my brother's leaving us for Margate I have sate at
times with Mrs. Sheridan, who is kind and considerate, so
that I have entire liberty. Her poor sister's children are all
with her. The girl gives her constant employment, and
seems to profit by being under so good an instructor. Their
father was here for some days, but I did not see him. Last
night Mrs. S. showed me a picture of Mrs. Tickell, which she
wears round her neck. . . . Dick is still in town, and we do
not expect him for some time. Mrs. Sheridan seems now
quite reconciled to those little absences which she knows are
unavoidable. I never saw any one so constant in employing
every moment of her time, and to that I attribute, in a great
measure, the recovery of her health and spirits. The education of her niece, her music, books, and work, occupy every
moment of the day. After dinner the children, who call her
mamma-aunt, spend some time with us, and her manner to
them is truly delightful."

Mrs. Tickell was Mrs. Sheridan's younger sister, and died just a year before her. In the meantime she had taken immediate charge of Tickell's motherless children, and the pretty "copy of verses" which she dedicated to her sister's memory embellishes and throws light upon her own.

> " The hours, the days pass on ; sweet spring returns,
> And whispers comfort to the heart that mourns
> But not to mine, whose dear and cherished grief
> Asks for indulgence, but ne'er hopes relief.
> For oh, can changing seasons e'er restore
> The lov'd companion I must still deplore ;
> Shall all the wisdom of the world combined
> Erase thy image, Mary, from my mind,
> Or bid me hope from others to receive
> The fond affection thou alone could'st give.
> Ah no, my best belov'd, thou still shalt be
> My friend, my sister, all the world to me.
>
> .   .   .   .
>
> " Oh, if the soul released from mortal cares
> Views the sad scene, the voice of mourning hears,
> Then, dearest saint, did'st thou thy heaven forego,
> Lingering on earth, in pity to our woe,
> 'Twas thy kind influence soothed our minds to peace,
> And bade our vain and selfish murmurs cease.
> 'Twas thy soft smile that gave the worshipped clay
> Of thy bright essence one celestial ray,
> Making e'en death so beautiful, that we
> Gazing on it, forgot our misery.
> Then—pleasing thought ! ere to the realms of light
> Thy franchised spirit took its happy flight,
> With fond regard perhaps thou saw'st me bend
> O'er the cold relics of my heart's best friend ;
> And heard'st me swear while her dear hand I prest,
> And tears of agony bedew'd my breast,
> For her lov'd sake to act the mother's part,

And take her darling infants to my heart,
With tenderest care their youthful minds improve,
And guard her treasure with protecting love ;
Once more look down, blest creature, and behold
These arms the precious innocents enfold.
Assist my erring nature to fulfil
The sacred trust and ward off every ill ;
And oh ! let *her* who is my dearest care,
Thy blest regard and heavenly influence share.
Teach me to form her pure and artless mind,
Like thine, as true, as innocent, as kind,
That when some future day my hopes shall bless,
And every voice her virtue shall express,
When my fond heart delighted hears her praise,
As with unconscious loveliness she strays,
Such, let me say with tears of joy the while,
Such was the softness of my Mary's smile.
Such was *her* youth, so blithe, so rosy-sweet,
And such *her* mind unpractised in deceit,
With artless eloquence, unstudied grace,
Thus did she gain in every heart a place.
Then while the dear remembrance I behold,
Time shall steal on, nor tell me I am old,
Till nature wearied, each fond duty o'er,
I join my angel friend to part no more !"

There is something extremely sweet and touching in
these lines, with their faded elegance, their pretty sentiment, the touch of the rococo in them which has now
recovered popular favour, something between poetry and
embroidery, and the most tender feminine feeling. All
sorts of pretty things were said of this gentle woman in
her day. Jackson of Exeter, the musician, who had some
professional engagements with her father, and accompanied
her often in her songs, said that " to see her as she stood
singing beside him at the pianoforte, was like looking
into the face of an angel." Another still higher authority,

the Bishop of Norwich, described her as "the connecting link between woman and angel." To Wilkes, the coarse and wild yet woman-loving demagogue, she was "the most modest flower he had ever seen." Sir Joshua painted her as St. Cecilia, and this was the flattering name by which she was known. Her letters, with a good deal of haste, and the faintest note of flippancy in them, are pretty too, full of news and society, and the card-tables at which she lost her money, and the children in whom her real heart was centred. The romantic girl had grown into a woman, not lofty or great, but sweet and clever, and silly and generous, a fascinating creature. Moore describes with a comical high-flown incongruity which reminds us of Mr. Micawber, her various qualities, the intellect which could appreciate the talents of her husband, the feminine sensibility that could passionately feel his success. "Mrs. Sheridan may well take her place beside these Roman wives," he says ; "not only did Calpurnia sympathise with the glory of her husband abroad, but she could also, like Mrs. Sheridan, *add a charm to his talents at home by setting his verses to music and singing* them to her harp." Poor Siren, she had her triumphs, but she had her troubles also, many and sore. In Professor Smyth's little book there is an account of a scene which, though it happened after her death, throws some light upon one side of her troubled existence. Smyth had been engaged as tutor to Tom after his mother's death, and this was one of the interferences which he had to submit to. Sheridan had been paying a hurried visit to the house at Wanstead in which Tom and his tutor lived :

" It was a severe frost, and had been long, when he came
one evening to dine, after his usual manner, on a boiled
chicken, at 7, 8, or 9 o'clock, just as it happened, and had
hardly drunk his claret, and got the room filled with wax lights,
without which he could not exist, when he sent for me ; and,
lo and behold, the business was that he was miserable on
account of Tom's being on the ice, that he would certainly be
drowned, etc., and that he begged it of me as the greatest
favour I could do him in some way or other to prevent it.
I expostulated with him—that I skated myself—that I had
a servant with a rope and ladder at the bank—that the ice
would now bear a waggon, etc. etc. ; and at last, seeing me
grow half angry at his unreasonableness, he acquiesced in
what I said, and calling his carriage, as he must be at Drury
Lane that night he said, (it was then eleven and he was nine
miles off), he withdrew.   In about half an hour afterwards,
as I was going to bed, I heard a violent ringing at the gate ;
I was wanted ; and sure enough what should I see, glaring
through the bars, and outshining the lamps of the carriage,
but the fine eyes of Sheridan.   'Now do not laugh at me,
Smyth,' he said, 'but I cannot rest or think of anything but
this d—d ice and this skating, and you must promise me
there shall be no more of it.'   I said what may be supposed ;
and in short was at last obliged to thrust my hand through
the bars, which he shook violently, in token that his wishes
should be obeyed.   'Never was such a nonsensical person as
this father of yours,' said I to Tom.   There was no difficulty
in coming to a common vote on that point ; and so, after
spending nearly an hour abusing him, half laughing and
half crying, for I was as fond of skating as my pupil could
be, lamenting our unhappy fate, we went to bed.   We sent
up various petitions and remonstrances while the frost lasted,
but all in vain.   'Have a glass case constructed for your son
at once,' said Mr. Grey to him—an observation which Tom
used to quote to me with particular approbation and delight.
I talked over the subject of Mr. Sheridan and his idle ner-
vousness with Mrs. Canning, who lived at the end of the
village.   She told me that nothing could be done—that he
would tease and irritate Mrs. Sheridan in this manner till she
was ready to dash her head against the wall, being of the

same temperament of genius as her husband : that she had
seen her burst into tears and leave the room ; then the scene
changed, and the wall seemed full as likely to receive his
head in turn.   The folly, however, Mrs. Canning said, was
not merely once and away, but was too often repeated ; and
Mrs. Canning used sometimes, as she told me, to be not a
little thankful that she was herself of a more ordinary clay,
and that the gods, as in the case of Audrey, had not made
her poetical."

This perhaps is the least comprehensible part of Sheridan's character.   The combination of this self-tormentor,
endowed with a faculty for extracting annoyance and
trouble out of every new turn in his circumstances,
and persecuting those who were dearest to him by his
caprices, with the reckless and careless man of pleasure,
is curious, and difficult to realise.

Mrs. Sheridan died in 1792.   She had been taken to
Bristol, in hopes that the change of air would do her
good.   But her time had come, and there was no hope
for her.   Her husband attended her with all the tenderness and anxiety which a man, no doubt remorseful,
always impressionable, and ready to be moved by the
sight, which was intolerable to him, of suffering—might
be supposed to feel, watching over her with the profoundest devotion.   "He cannot bear to think her in
danger," writes a sympathetic friend, "or that any one
else should ; though he is as attentive and watchful as if
he expected every moment to be her last.   It is impossible for any man to behave with greater tenderness or
to feel more on such an occasion."   He was at her bed-
side night and day, "and never left her one moment that
could be avoided."   The crisis was one in which with
his readiness of emotion, and quick and sure response to

M

all that touched him, he was sure to appear well. Moore
found, among the mass of documents through which he
had to pick his way, a scrap of paper evidently belonging to this period, which gives strange expression to that
realistic and materialistic horror of death as death, which
was one of the features of the time.   "The loss of the
breath from a beloved object long suffering in pain and
certainty to die, is not so great a privation as the last
loss of her beautiful remains if they remain so.   The
victory of the grave is sharper than the sting of death."
There is something in this sentiment which makes us
shudder.   That crowning pang of separation,—

> "Our lives have fallen so far apart
> We cannot hear each other speak,"—

does not strike this mourner.   The contact of the
body and decay, the loss of "the beautiful remains," is
what moves him.   It is like a child's primitive horror
of the black box and the deep hole.   In his own dying
hour an awe unspeakable stole over his face when he was
informed that a clergyman had been sent for.   These
were things to be held at arm's length ; when he was
compulsorily brought in contact with them, the terror
was almost greater than the anguish.

The Linley family had suffered terribly in these
years, one following another to the grave.   There is a
most touching description of the father given by the
actress Mrs. Crouch, which goes direct to the heart—

"After Miss Marion Linley died, it was melancholy for
her to sing to Mr. Linley, whose tears continually fell on the
keys as he accompanied her ; and if in the course of her profession she was obliged to practise a song which he had been
accustomed to hear his lost daughter sing, the similarity of

their manner and voices, which he had once remarked with
pleasure, then affected him to such a degree that he was frequently forced to quit his instrument and walk about the room
to recover his composure."

After his wife's death, Sheridan's life assumed another
phase. He had no longer the anchor, such as it was,
which steadied him—not even the tug of remorse to
bring him home to a house where there was now no
one waiting for him. We are indebted to Professor
Smyth's narrative for a very graphic description of this
portion of Sheridan's life. In the very formation of
their connection, the peculiarities of his future employer
were at once made known to him. It was appointed
that he should meet Sheridan at dinner in town to
conclude the arrangement about the tutorship, and to
keep this appointment he came up specially from the
country. The dinner hour was seven, but at nine Smyth
and the friend who was to introduce him ate their cold
meal without Sheridan, who then sent to say that he
had been detained at the House, but would sup with
them at midnight at the St. Alban's Tavern, whither
they resorted with precisely the same result. Next day,
however, the meeting did take place, and the ruffled soul
of the young scholar, who had been extremely indignant
to find himself thus treated, was soothed in a few minutes
by the engaging manner and delightful speech of his patron.
It was at Isleworth, Sheridan's country house, that they
met, where very lately Madame de Genlis, that interesting and sentimental refugee, with her lovely daughter
Pamela, the beautiful young creature whom Mrs. Sheridan
had bidden Lord Edward Fitzgerald to marry when she
died, had paid him a visit. The house was dirty and

desolate, the young observer thought, but the master of
it the most captivating of men. His brilliant and ex-
pressive eyes, a certain modesty in his manner, for which
the young Don was not prepared, struck Smyth above all :
and he in his turn pleased the nervous and troubled
father, who would have kept young Tom in a glass case
had he dared. Afterwards another house was taken in
Wanstead, in order that Sheridan's baby daughter might
be placed under the charge of Mrs. Canning, the lady
who had nursed Mrs. Sheridan and loved her, and who
lived in this village ; and here the boy and his tutor were
sent. But a very short time after another blow fell upon
Sheridan in the person of this child, whom Professor
Smyth describes as the loveliest child he ever saw—an
exceptional creature, whom Sheridan made a little goddess
of, worshipping her with every baby rite that could be
thought of. One night the house had awoke to unwonted
merriment ; a large childish party filled the rooms, and
dancing was going on merrily, when Mrs. Canning suddenly flung open the door, crying out, " The child, the
child is dying ! " Sheridan's grief was intense and overwhelming : it was piteous to hear his moans during the
terrible night that followed. His warm-hearted emotional
being, horrified and panic-stricken by the approach of
death, was once more altogether overwhelmed. The
cruel climax of blow after blow crushed him to the earth.

During this time his parliamentary life was going on
with interruptions, sometimes brightening into flashes of
his pristine brilliancy. But at this moment there were
other troubles besides those of his home and heart, to
make his attendance irregular and withdraw his thoughts
from public affairs. How the theatre had been going on

all this time it is difficult to make out. We are told of
endless embarrassments, difficulties, and trouble, of a
treasury emptied wantonly, and actors left without their
pay,—of pieces which failed and audiences which diminished. But, on the other hand, we are informed that the
prosperity of Drury Lane never was greater than during
this period, while the old theatre lasted; and, as it was
the only source from which Sheridan drew his income, it
is very evident that, notwithstanding all irregularities,
broken promises, crowds of duns, and general mismanage-
ment, there was an unfailing fountain of money to be
drawn upon. The whole story is confused. We are
sometimes told that he was himself the manager, and it
is certain that now and then he stooped even so far as
to arrange a pantomime; while at the same time we
find the theatre under the management of King at one
time, of Kemble at another, men much better qualified
than Sheridan. The mere fact indeed that the Kemble
family was at that time on the boards of Drury Lane
would seem a sufficient proof of the success of the theatre;
but the continually recurring discovery that the proprietor's pressing necessities had cleared the treasury
altogether was little likely to keep the troupe together
or inspire its efforts. When any influential member of the
company became unmanageable on this score, Sheridan's
persuasive talent was called in to make all right. Once,
we are told, Mrs. Siddons, who had declared that she
would not act until her salary was paid, who had resisted
successively the eloquent appeals of her colleagues and
the despair of the manager, and was calmly sewing
at home after the curtain had risen for the piece in
which she was expected to perform, yielded help-

lessly when Sheridan himself, all suave and irresistible, came on the scene, and suffered herself to be driven to the theatre like a lamb. On another occasion it was Kemble that rebelled. We are tempted to quote, for its extremely ludicrous character, this droll little scene. Sheridan had come in accidentally to join the party in the green room after the performance, and, taking his seat at the table, made as usual a cheerful beginning of conversation. Kemble, however, would make no reply.

"The great actor now looked unutterable things, and occasionally emitted a humming sound like that of a bee, and groaned in spirit inwardly. A considerable time elapsed, and frequent repetitions of the sound, when at length, like a pillar of state, up rose Kemble, and in these words addressed the astonished proprietor : 'I am an EAGLE, whose wings have been bound down by frosts and snows, but now I shake my pinions and cleave into the genial air into which I was born !' He then deliberately resumed his seat, as if he had relieved himself from unsupportable thraldom."

Undaunted by this solemn address, Sheridan drew his chair closer, and at the end of the prolonged sitting left the place, not too steadily it is to be feared, arm in arm with the exasperated eagle, whom he had made as mild as any mouse. He did many feats of the same kind. Once, the bankers having sternly resisted all blandishments of manager, treasurer, all the staff of the theatre, Sheridan went in gaily to the charge, and returned in a few minutes beaming and successful, with the money they wanted. When he chose, nobody could stand against him.

Poor Mr. Smyth had a terrible life of it with this disorderly patron. His letters were neglected, his ap-

pointments broken, his salary left unpaid. Once his
pupil Tom was sent for in hot haste to meet his father
at a certain roadside inn, and there waited for days if not
weeks in vain expectation of his errant parent, leaving the
unfortunate preceptor a prey to all kinds of anxiety.
Another time the long-suffering Smyth was left at Bognor
with an old servant, Martha, without money, or occupation, waiting for a summons to London which never
came ; and, unable at last to live any longer on credit,
after letters innumerable of entreaty, protestation, and
wrath, went up to London full of fury, determined to
endure no more ; but was met by Sheridan with such
cordial pleasure, surprise that he had not come sooner,
and satisfaction with his appearance now, since Tom was
getting into all sorts of mischief—that the angry tutor
was entirely vanquished, and remorseful when he thought
of the furious letter he had sent to this kind friend.
What followed is worth quoting.

"'I wrote you a letter lately,' I said ; 'it was an angry
one. You will be so good as to think no more of it.' 'Oh,
certainly not, my dear Smyth,' he said, 'I shall never think
of what you have said in it, be assured ;' and, putting his
hand in his pocket, 'here it is,' he said, offering it to me. I
was glad enough to get hold of it, but looking at it as I was
about to throw it into the fire, lo, and behold, I saw that it
had never been opened !"

Such exasperating yet ludicrous incidents were now
commonplaces of Sheridan's life. "Intercourse with
him," says Professor Smyth in a harsher mood, moved
by some sting of bitter recollection, "was one eternal
insult, mortification, and disappointment." There was a
bag on his table into which all letters were stuffed indis-

criminately, and in which, when it was turned out, an astonished applicant for debt or favour might see a succession of his own letters as he sent them, with not one seal broken; but to lessen the mortification would find also letters enclosing money sent in answer to Sheridan's own urgent applications, turned out in the same condition, having been stuffed with the rest into that hopeless waste heap. When Professor Smyth appealed to Sheridan's old servant to know if nothing could be done to remedy this, Edwards told him a piteous story of how he had found Mr. Sheridan's window, which rattled, wedged up with bank-notes, which the muddled reveller, returning late at night, had stuffed into the gaping sash, out of his pocket. The story altogether is laughable and pitiful, a tragic comedy of the most woeful fooling. He had no longer youth enough to warrant an easy laugh, his reputation was going from him. He was harassed by endless creditors and duns, not able to stir out of his house without encountering two or three waiting to waylay him. The first of these, if he caught Sheridan at a moment when his pocket had just been replenished, would get the amount of his bill in full, whatever the others might have to say. The stories are endless which deal with these embarrassments, and the shifts and devices of the struggling man were endless also. They are very ridiculous to hear of, but how humiliating, miserable, and sickening to the heart and mind all these repetitions must have been! And then to make everything worse the poor old theatre fell to pieces, and the taste of the day demanded a costly and luxurious new building, according to improved fashions. The money to do this

was raised by the manufacture of new shares, in which
there was no difficulty—but which naturally restricted
the after profits of the original proprietors. And what
was still more serious, the interval occupied in the
rebuilding—during which time their profits may be said
to have ceased altogether—and the excess of the cost
over the estimate, made an enormous difference to men
who had no reserve to fall back upon. The company
in the meantime played in a small theatre at a great
expense, and Sheridan, profuse and lavish, unable to
retrench, not wise enough even to attempt retrenchment,
got deeper and deeper into debt and embarrassment.

Besides all these misadventures a new and malign
influence now got possession of him. He had been presented to the young Prince of Wales, at a time when that
illustrious personage was still little more than a boy, and
full, it was believed, of promise and hopefulness: and had
gradually grown to be one of the most intimate habitués
of his society, a devoted retainer, adviser, and defender,
holding by him in all circumstances, and sharing the
irregularities of his life, and the horseplay of his amuse-
ments. The *Octogenarian*, from whose rather foolish
book we have occasionally quoted, gives a tissue of
absurd stories, professedly heard from Sheridan's own
lips, in which the adventures of a night are recorded,
and the heir-apparent is represented to us in company
with two statesmen, as all but locked up for the night at
a police station. Whether this was true or not, it is
certain that the glamour which there is in the rank of a
royal personage, that dazzlement which so few can resist,
fell upon Sheridan. His action as the adviser and representative in Parliament of this unillustrious Prince was

dignified and sensible, but the orgies of Carlton House were unfortunately too much in Sheridan's way to be restrained or discountenanced by him, and so much hope and possibility as remained in his life was lost in the vulgar dissipations of this depraved secondary court, and in the poor vanity of becoming boon companion and buffoon to that first gentleman in Europe, whose florid and padded comeliness was the admiration of his day. It was a poor end for the great dramatist, who has kept thousands of his countryfolk in genial, not uninnocent amusement for the last century, and for the great orator whose eloquence had disturbed the judgment of the most august of legislative assemblies, and shaken even the convictions of the hottest partisans; but it was an end to which he had been for some time tending, and which perhaps the loss of his wife had made one way or other inevitable.

In the meantime several events occurred which may fill up this division of the life of the man as apart from that of the politician and orator. In 1794 the new theatre was finished, and Sheridan sketched out for the opening a sort of extravaganza called *The Glorious First of June*, which was apparently in celebration of the naval victory of Lord Howe. The dialogue was not his, but merely the construction and arrangement, and in emulation of Tilbury and the feats of Mr. Puff, a grand sea-fight, with finale of a lovers' meeting to the triumphant sounds of "Rule Britannia," was introduced. The two pasteboard fleets rehearsed their manoeuvres under the eye of the Duke of Clarence, and it is to be supposed that the spectacle had a triumphant success. A year or two later a less agreeable incident occurred in the history of

Drury Lane. Either deceived by the many who were ready to stake their credit upon the authenticity of the Ireland forgeries—then given forth as a discovery of precious relics of Shakespeare, including among them a completed and unpublished play—or deceived in his own person on the subject, one on which he was not learned, Sheridan accepted for the theatre this play, called *Vortigern*, and produced it with much pomp and magnificence. The audience was a crowded and critical one, and the public mind was so strongly roused by the question, that no doubt there was some factious feeling in the prompt and unmistakable rejection of the false Shakespeare, to which Kemble by his careless acting is said to have contributed. He had never believed in the discovery, and might be irritated that the decision had been made without consulting him. Dr. Parr, however, for whom Sheridan had a great respect, and with whom he kept up friendly relations all his life, was one of those who had headed the blunder, receiving the forgeries reverentially as pure Shakespeare ; and it was natural enough that Sheridan's judgment should have been influenced by a man whom he must have felt a much better authority on the question than himself. For he was no student of Shakespeare, and his prevailing recklessness was more than enough to counterbalance the keen critical instinct which produced the *Critic*. In all likelihood he never investigated the question at all, but calculated on a temporary theatrical success, without other results. "Sheridan was never known to offer his opinion on the matter until after its representation on the stage : he left the public to decide on its merits," says one of his biographers : but the incident is not an agreeable one.

It was less his fault than that of his public, perhaps, that
the stage, shortly after recovering from the salutary influence of the *Critic*, dropped again into bathos and the false
heroic.   " Kotzebue and German sausages are the order of
the day," Sheridan himself is reported to have said when,
with a shrug of his shoulders, he produced the *Stranger*,
that culmination of the sentimental commonplace.   Everybody will remember Thackeray's delightful banter of this
wonderful production, which has, however, situations so
skilfully prepared and opportunities so great for a clever
actress, that it has continued to find a place in the repertory of most theatres, and is still to be heard of as the
show-piece of a wandering company, as well as now and
then on the most ambitious boards, its dubious moral and
un-English *dénouement* notwithstanding.   With Mrs. Siddons as Mrs. Haller, it may be imagined that the real
pathos involved in the story would have full expression.

The success of the *Stranger* impelled Sheridan to
another adaptation of a similar kind, in the tragedy of
Pizarro, which he altered and decorated so much, it is
said, as to make it almost his own.   The bombast and
claptrap of this production make us regret to associate it
with his name, but here also the dramatic construction
was good enough and the situations so striking as to rivet
the attention of the audience, while the high-flown magnificence of the sentiments was such as always delights the
multitude.   When something was said to Pitt, between
whom and Sheridan a gradually increasing enmity had
grown, about the new drama, the minister answered, "If
you mean what Sheridan wrote, there is nothing new in
it.   I have heard it all long ago in his speeches on
Hastings' trial."   It is undeniable that there is a good

deal of truth in this, and that Rolla's grand patriotic
tirade which used to be in all school reading-books, as a
lesson in elocution, bears a strong resemblance to many
passages in Sheridan's speeches.   All this helped its
popularity.   Grand addresses in favour of patriotism are
always delightful to the galleries, and have at all times
a charm for the general imagination : but in those days
when there was actual fighting going on, and France, who
had constituted herself the pedagogue of the world, to
teach the nations the alphabet of freedom, was supposed
to threaten and endanger England with her fiery teaching,
it may be supposed to what a height of enthusiasm these
exhortations would raise the audience.   "They follow
an adventurer whom they fear, and obey a power which
they hate ; we revere a monarch whom we love, a God
whom we adore.   They boast they come but to improve
our State, enlarge our thoughts, and free us from the
yoke of error !   Yes ! they will give enlightened freedom
to our minds, who are themselves the slaves of passion,
avarice, and pride !"   Whether it were under Robespierre
or Bonaparte, the common people in England scorned
and feared the heated neighbour-nation which thought
itself entitled to dictate to the world ; and no doubt the
popular mind made a rapid adaptation of these heroic
phrases.

It had been hard to move the author to complete the
Critic. and the reader will remember the trick of Linley
and his coadjutors in those early days when the delays
and evasions of the gay young man were an excellent
jest, and their certainty of being able to put all right
when they could lock him in with his work, had something
triumphant in it.   But all that was over now ; old Linley

was dead, and a new generation who had no worship for
Sheridan, and a very clear apprehension of the everlasting
confusion produced by his disorderly ways, had taken the
place of the light-hearted actors of old.   But notwithstanding the awe-inspiring presence of Mrs. Siddons, and
the importance of her brother, the astounding fact that
when the curtain fell upon the fourth act of *Pizarro*, these
theatrical potentates had not yet seen their parts for the
fifth, which they had to study in the interval, is vouched
for by various witnesses.   It is hard to imagine the state
of the actors' minds, the terrible anxiety of the manager
in such an extraordinary dilemma, and still more hard to
realise the hopeless confusion in the mind of the man who
knew all that was being risked by such a piece of folly,
and yet could not nerve himself to the work till the last
moment.   He was drifting on the rapids by this time,
and going headlong to ruin, heedless of everything, name
and fame, credit and fortune, the good opinion of his
friends, the support of the public, all except the indulgence of the whim of the moment, or of the habit which
was leading him to destruction.

He took another step about the same time which
might perhaps have redeemed him had it been more
wisely set about.   He had met one evening, so the
story goes, among other more important, and let us
hope more well-bred people, a foolish, pretty girl, who
either out of flippant dislike to his looks, or that very
transparent *agacerie* by which foolish men are sometimes attracted in the lower ranks of life, regarded him
with exclamations of "fright! horrid creature!" and the
like, something in the style not of Evelina, but of Miss
Burney's vulgar personages.   He was by this time forty-

four, but ready enough still to take up any such
challenge, and either he was piqued into making so
frank a critic change her opinions, or the prettiness and
foolishness of the girl amused and pleased him. He set
to work at once to make her aware that a man of middle-
age and unhandsome aspect may yet outdo the youngest
and most attractive, and no very great time elapsed
before he was completely successful. The lady's father
was little pleased with the match. He was a clergyman,
the Dean of Winchester, and might well have been indis-
posed to give his daughter and her five thousand pounds
to a man with such a reputation. He made his consent
conditional on the settling of fifteen thousand pounds, in
addition to her own little fortune, upon her. Sheridan
had always been great in financial surprises, and to the
astonishment of the dean, the fifteen thousand was soon
forthcoming. He got it this time by new shares of the
theatre, thus diminishing his receipts always a little
and a little more. A small estate, Polesden, in Surrey,
was bought with the money, and for a time all was
gaiety and pleasure. It was in order to tell him of
this marriage that Sheridan sent for his son, from his
tutor and his lessons, on the occasion already referred to,
to meet him at Guildford at an inn of which he had forgotten the name. Four or five days after, the anxious
tutor received a letter from Tom. "My father I have
never seen," wrote the lad, "and all that I can hear of
him is that instead of dining with me on Wednesday
last, he passed through Guildford on his way to town
with four horses and lamps, about twelve." Like father
like son, the youth had remained there, though with
only a few shillings in his pockets : but at the end was

so "bored and wearied out" that he would have been
glad to return even to his books.   Finally, he was sent
for to London and informed of the mystery.   His letter
to Smyth disclosing this is so characteristic that it is
worth quoting :—

> "It is not I that am to be married, nor you.   Set your
> heart at rest : it is my father himself ; the lady a Miss Ogle,
> who lives at Winchester ; and that is the history of the
> Guildford business.   About my own age—better me to marry
> her, you will say.   I am not of that opinion.   My father
> talked to me two hours last night, and made out to me
> that it was the most sensible thing he could do.   Was not
> this very clever of him ?   Well, my dear Mr. S., you should
> have been tutor to him, you see.   I am incomparably the
> most rational of the two."

Moore describes the immediate result of the new marriage as a renewal of Sheridan's youth.   "It is said by
those who were in habits of intimacy with him at this
period that they had seldom seen his spirits in a state of
more buoyant vivacity," and there was perhaps a possibility that the new event might have proved a turning
point.   It is unfair to blame the foolish girl, who had no
idea what the dangers were which she had so rashly
undertaken to deal with, that she did not reclaim or
deliver Sheridan.   To do this was beyond her power as
it was beyond his own.

CHAPTER VI.

DECADENCE.

SHERIDAN'S parliamentary career was long, and he took an important part in much of the business of the country; but he never struck again the same high note as that with which he electrified the House on the question of the impeachment of Warren Hastings. His speech in answer to Lord Mornington's denunciation of the revolution in France, perhaps his next most important effort, was eloquent and striking, but it had not the glow and glitter of the great oration under which the Commons of England held their breath. The French Revolution by this time had ceased to be the popular and splendid outburst of freedom which it had at first appeared. Opinions were now violently divided. The recent atrocities in France had scared England; and all the moving subjects which had inspired Sheridan before, the pictures of innocence outraged and the defenceless slaughtered, were now in the hands of his political opponents. He selected skilfully, however, the points which he could most effectively turn against them, and seizing upon Lord Mornington's description of the sacrifices by which French patriotism was compelled to prove itself, the compulsory loans and

N

services, the privations and poverty amid which the
leaders of the revolution were struggling, drew an effective
picture of the very different state of affairs in England,
which throws a curious light upon the political condition
of the time. Sheridan's party had suffered many losses
and defections. A peer in those days or a wealthy
landed gentleman, had need to be enlightened and strong-
minded indeed, if not almost fanatical in opinion, to
continue cordially on the side of those who were con-
fiscating and murdering his equals on the other side of
the Channel, and who had made the very order to which
he belonged an offence against the State. The Whig
nobility were no more stoical or heroic than other men,
and the publication of Burke's *Reflections* and his impassioned testimony against the uncontrollable tendencies
of the revolution had moved them profoundly even before
the course of events proved his prophecies true. To
make the conversion of these important adherents more
easy, Pitt, on the other hand, held out his arms to them,
and, as the fashion of the time was, posts and sinecures
of all kinds rained upon the new converts. Sheridan,
with instinctive perception of the mode of attack which
suited his powers best, seized upon this with something
of the same fervour as that with which, though in no
way particularly interested in India, he had seized upon
the story of the injured Begums and cruel English con-
querors in the East. It was altogether the other side of
the argument, yet the inspiration of the orator was the
same. It was now the despoilers who were his clients :
but their work of destruction had not been to their own
profit. They were sufferers not gainers. No rich posts nor
hidden treasures were reserved by them for themselves,

and the contrast between the advantages reaped by so many Englishmen arrayed against them, and the sacrifices and privations of the French patriots, was perfect. Sheridan took up the subject with all the greater wealth and energy of indignant conviction that he himself had never reaped any substantial advantage from the occasional elevation of his own party. He had carried no spoils with him out of office ; he had not made hay while the sun shone. If anybody had a right to be called a disinterested politician he had, in this sense at least. His interest in the subjects which he treated might be more a party interest than any real devotion to the cause of freedom and humanity ; but his hands were clean from bribe or pecuniary inducement ; and his fervour, if perhaps churned up a little by party motives, was never ungenerous. The indignant bitterness with which he and the small party who adhered to Fox regarded the desertion of so many of their supporters, gave force to the reply with which he met Lord Mornington's unlucky description of the French efforts. On no other point could the comparison have been so completely in favour of the revolutionary. Sheridan takes the account of their privations triumphantly out of the hand of the narrator. Far different indeed, he cries scornfully, is the position of the rival statesmen and officials in England. He can imagine the address made to them "by our prudent minister " in words like the following, words which burn and sting with all the fire of satire—

" Do I demand of you wealthy citizens (it is Pitt who is supposed to be the speaker) to lend your hoards to Government without interest ?   On the contrary, when I shall come to propose a loan, there is not a man of you to whom I shall

not hold out at least a job in every part of the subscription,
and a usurious profit upon every pound you devote to the necessities of your country.   Do I demand of you, my fellow-place-
men and brother-pensioners, that you should sacrifice any part
of your stipends to the public exigency ?   On the contrary,
am I not daily insuring your emoluments, and your numbers
in proportion as the country becomes unable to provide for
you ?   Do I require of you my latest and most zealous pro-
selytes, of you who have come over to me for the special
purpose of supporting the war, a war on the success of which
you solemnly protest that the salvation of Britain and of civil
society itself depends,—do I require of you that you should
make a temporary sacrifice in the cause of human nature of
the greater part of your private incomes ?   No, gentlemen, I
scorn to take advantage of the eagerness of your zeal ; and to
prove that I think the sincerity of your attachment to me
needs no such test I will make your interest co-operate with
your principle ; I will quarter many of you on the public
supply instead of calling on you to contribute to it, and
while their whole thoughts are absorbed in patriotic appre-
hensions for their country, I will dexterously force upon
others the favourite objects of the vanity or ambition of
their lives."

Then the orator turns to give his own judgment of
the state of affairs.   "Good God, sir," he cries, "that he
should have thought it prudent to have forced this contrast upon our attention," and he hurries on with indignant eloquence to describe the representations made of
"the unprecedented peril of the country," the constitution
in danger, the necessity of "maintaining the war by every
possible sacrifice," and that the people should not murmur
at their burdens, seeing that their all was at stake—

" The time is come when all honest and disinterested men
should rally round the throne as round a standard—for what ?
Ye honest and disinterested men to receive, for your own
private emolument, a portion of those very taxes which they

themselves wring from the people on the pretence of saving
them from the poverty and distress which you say the enemy
would inflict, but which you take care no enemy shall be
able to aggravate. Oh, shame ! shame ! is this a time for
selfish intrigues, and the little dirty traffic for lucre and
emolument ? Does it suit the honour of a gentleman to ask
at such a moment ? Does it become the honesty of a minister to grant ? Is it intended to confirm the pernicious
doctrine, so industriously propagated by many, that all public
men are impostors, and that every politician has his price ?
Or even where there is no principle in the bosom, why does
not prudence hint to the mercenary and the vain to abstain
a while at least, and wait the fitting of the times ? Improvident impatience ! Nay, even from those who seem to have
no direct object of office or profit, what is the language
which the actors speak ? The Throne is in danger ! we
will support the Throne : but let us share the smiles of
royalty ; the order of nobility is in danger. ' I will fight
for nobility,' says the viscount, ' but my zeal would be
much greater if I were made an earl.' ' Rouse all the marquis
within me,' exclaims the earl, ' and the peerage never turned
forth a more undaunted champion in its cause than I shall
prove.' ' Stain my green ribbon blue,' cries out the illustrious knight, ' and the fountain of honour will have a fast
and faithful servant.' "

This scathing blast of satire must, one would think,
have overwhelmed the Whig deserters, the new placemen
and sinecurists, though it could not touch the impassioned soul of such a prophet as Burke, whose denuncia-
tions and anticipations had been so terribly verified.
The reader already acquainted with the life of Burke
will remember how, early in the controversy, before
France had stained her first triumphs, Sheridan lost,
on account of his continued faith in the Revolution,
the friendship of his great countryman, whose fiery
temper was unable to brook so great a divergence of

opinion, and who cut him sternly off, as he afterwards
did a more congenial and devoted friend, Fox, by
whom the breach was acknowledged with tears in a
scene as moving as ever was enacted in the House
of Commons.   Sheridan did not feel it so deeply,
the link between them being lighter, and the position of involuntary rivalship almost inevitable.   And
though it cannot be believed that his convictions on
the subject were half so profound, or his judgment so
trustworthy, his was the more difficult side of opinion,
and his fidelity to the cause, which politically and we
may even say conventionally, was that of freedom, was
unwavering.   The speech from which we have quoted
could not, from its nature, be so carefully premeditated
and prepared, as Sheridan's great efforts had heretofore
been ; but it had the advantage of being corrected for
the press, and has consequently reached us in a fuller
and more complete form than any other of Sheridan's
speeches.   Professor Smyth gives a graphic account of
his sudden appearance at Wanstead along with the editor
of the paper in which it had been reported, and of the
laborious diligence with which he devoted himself to its
revision, during several days of unbroken work.   But
we should scarcely have known our Sheridan had not
this spasmodic effort been balanced by an instance of
characteristic indolence and carelessness.   Lord Mornington in his speech had made much reference to a
French pamphlet by Brissot, a translation of which had
been republished in London, with a preface by Burke,
and largely circulated.   Smyth remarked that Sheridan
accepted Lord M.'s view of this pamphlet, and his quo-
tations from it.   " How could I do otherwise ?" he said.

"I never read a word of it." Perhaps it was not
necessary. The careful combination of facts and details
was not in Sheridan's way; but in his haphazard daring
a certain instinct guided him, and he seized unerringly
the thing he could do, the point of the position, picturesque and personal, which his faculty could best
assail.

A far less satisfactory chapter in his life was that
already referred to, which linked Sheridan's fortunes
with those of the Prince Regent, and made him, for
a long time, almost the representative in Parliament
of that royal personage. When the first illness of
the King, in 1789, made it likely that power must
come one way or other into the hands of the heir-
apparent, there was much excitement, as was natural,
among the party with which the name of the Prince
of Wales was connected, and who, as appeared, had
everything to hope from his accession, actual or virtual.
It is scarcely necessary to our purpose to trace the stormy
party discussions on the subject of the Regency, between
the extreme claim put forth by Fox of the right of the
Prince to be immediately invested with all the powers of
royalty as his father's natural deputy and representative,
and the equally extreme counter-statement of Pitt, dictated by alarm as the other was by hope, that "the
Prince of Wales had no more right to exercise the powers
of government than any other person in the realm."
Sheridan's share in the debate was chiefly signalised by
his threat, as injudicious as the original assertion of his
leader, that the Prince might be provoked to make the
claim which the other party opposed so strenuously;"
"but his most important agency," says Moore, "lay

in the less public business connected with" the question. He was in high favour at Carlton House, and the chosen adviser of the Prince: and although Moore's researches enabled him to prove that the most important document in the whole episode—the Prince's letter to Pitt—was the production not of Sheridan but of the master-spirit Burke, Sheridan's pen was employed in various papers of importance; and though the post allotted to him in the shortlived new ministry was no more than that of Treasurer of the Navy, a position not at all adequate to his apparent importance, he was in reality a very active agent behind the scenes. The king's speedy recovery, however, at this moment was fatal to Sheridan's fortunes, and all that came of this momentary gleam of advancement to his family was that Charles Sheridan in Ireland, whose post had been the only gain of his brother's former taste of power, lost it in consequence of the new re-revolution of affairs, though he carried with him a pension of £1200 a year, probably a very good substitute. He was the only one profited in pocket by Sheridan's political elevation and fame. Once more, in 1806, after the death of Pitt, Sheridan followed Fox into office in the same unimportant post of Treasurer to the Navy. But Fortune was not on his side, and Fox's death in a few months withdrew him for ever from all the chances of power.

It seems inconceivable though true that the two great orators of the period, the men whose figures stand prominent in every discussion, and one of whom at least had so large and profound an influence on his time, should, when their party rose to the head of affairs, have been so unceremoniously disposed of. Sheridan's insig-

nificant post might be accounted for by his known
incapacity for continued exertion ; but to read the name
of Burke as Paymaster of the Forces, fills the reader
with amazement. They were both self-made, without
family or connections to found a claim upon, but the
eminence, especially of the latter, was incontestable.
Both were of the highest importance to their party,
and Sheridan was in the enjoyment of that favour of the
Prince which told for so much in those days. And yet
this was the best that their claims could secure. It is
a somewhat humiliating proof of how little great mental
gifts, reaching the height of genius in one case, can
do for their possessor. Both Burke and Sheridan are
favourite instances of the reverse opinion. It is a
commonplace to quote them as examples of the manner
in which a man of genius may raise himself to the
highest elevation. And yet after they had dazzled
England for years, one of them the highest originating
soul, the profoundest thinker of his class, the other an
unrivalled instrument at least in the hand of a great party
leader, this was all they could attain to — Edmund
Burke, Paymaster of the Forces; Brinsley Sheridan,
Treasurer of the Navy. It is a curious commentary
upon the unbounded applause and reputation which these
two men enjoyed in their day, and the place they have
taken permanently in the history of their generation.

Sheridan's connection with the Prince lasted for many
years. He appears to have been not only one of his
favourite companions, but for some time at least his
most confidential adviser. When the Prince on his
marriage put forth a second demand for the payment of
his debts, after the distinct promise made on the first

occasion that no such claim should be made again, it
was Sheridan who was the apologist, if apology his
explanation can be called.   He informed the House
that he had advised the Prince to make no such
pledge, but that it was inserted without the knowledge
of either, and at a moment when it was impossible to
withdraw from it.   He added that he himself had
drawn up a scheme of retrenchment which would have
made such an application unnecessary, that he had put a
stop to a loan proposed to be raised for the Prince in
France as unconstitutional, and that he had systematically
counselled an abstinence from all meddling in great political questions.   Moore characterises this explanation as
marked by "a communicativeness that seemed hardly
prudent," and it is difficult to suppose that Sheridan's
royal patron could have liked it; but he did not disown
it in any way, and retained the speaker in his closest
confidence for many years, during which Sheridan's time
and pen and ready eloquence were always at his master's
service.   There is a strange mixture throughout his
history of serviceableness and capacity for work, with
an almost incredible carelessness and indolence, of which
his behaviour at this period affords a curious example.
He would seem to have spared no trouble in the Prince's
service, to have been ready at his call at all times and
seasons, conducting the most important negotiations for
him, and acting as the means of communication between
him and the leaders of his party.   Perhaps pride and
a gratified sense of knowing the mind of the heir-
apparent better than any one else, may have supplied
the place of true energy and diligence for the moment;
and certainly he was zealous and busy in his patron's

affairs, disorderly and indifferent as he was in his own. And though his power and influence were daily decreasing in Parliament, his attendance becoming more and more irregular, and his interest in public business capricious and fitful, yet there were still occasions on which Sheridan came to the front with an energy and spirit worthy of his best days. One of these was at the time of the great mutiny at the Nore, when the ministry was embarrassed on all hands, the opposition violently factious, and every appearance alarming. Sheridan threw himself into the midst of the excitement with a bold and generous support of the Government which strengthened their hands in the emergency and did much to restore tranquillity and confidence. "The patriotic promptitude of his interference," says Moore, "was even more striking than it appears in the record of his Parliamentary labours." By this time Fox had withdrawn from the House, and no other of the Whig leaders showed anything of Sheridan's energy and public spirit. At a still later period, in the course of a discussion on the army estimates, he was complimented by Canning as "a man who had often come forward in times of public embarrassment as the champion of the country's rights and interests, and had rallied the hearts and spirits of the nation." The warmest admirer of Sheridan might be content to let such words as these stand as the conclusion of his parliamentary career.

Thus his life was chequered with bursts of recovery, with rapid and unexpected manifestations of power. Now and then he would rise to the height of a crisis, and by moments display a faculty prompt and eager and practical. Sometimes, on a special occasion, he would work

hard, "till the motes were in his eyes." There must have
been in him some germ of financial genius which enabled
him without any capital to acquire great property, and
conduct what was in reality a large commercial speculation
in his theatre with success for many years. All these
qualities are strangely at variance with the background of
heedlessness, indolence, and reckless self-indulgence which
take both credit and purpose out of his life. He is like
two men, one of them painfully building up what the
other every day delights to pull down. His existence
from the time of his wife's death seems, when we look
back upon it, like a headlong rush to destruction ; and
yet even in the last chapter of his career there were times
when he would turn and stand and present a manful front
to fate. Though there is no appearance in anything he
says or does of very high political principles, yet he held
steadfastly by the cause of reform, and for the freedom
of the subject, and against all encroachments of power,
as long as he lived. He was on the side of Ireland in
the troubles then as always existing, though of a
changed complexion from those we are familiar with
now. He would not allow himself to be persuaded
out of his faith in the new principle of freedom in
France, either by the excesses which disgraced it, or
by the potent arguments of his friend and countryman. And he was disinterested and faithful in his
party relations, giving up office almost unnecessarily
when he considered that his political allegiance required
it, and holding fast to his leader even when there was
estrangement between them. All these particulars should
be remembered to Sheridan's credit. He got nothing
for his political services, at a time when sinecures were

common, and, with one exception, kept his political
honour stainless, and never departed from his standard.

He served the Prince in the same spirit of disinterestedness—a disinterestedness so excessive that it looks
like recklessness and ostentatious indifference to ordinary
motives : that gratification in the confidence of royalty,
which in all ages has moved men to sacrifices and labours
not undertaken willingly in any other cause, seems a
poor sort of inspiration when Royal George was the
object of it ; but in this case it was like master like man,
and the boon companion whose wit enlivened the royal
orgies was not likely perhaps to judge his Prince by any
high ideal.   He had never received from his royal friend
" so much as the present of a horse or a picture," until in
the year 1804 the appointment of Receiver of the Duchy
of Cornwall was conferred upon him, an appointment
which he announces to the then minister, Mr. Addington,
with lively satisfaction and gratitude.

"It has been my pride and pleasure," he says, "to have
exerted my humble efforts to serve the Prince without ever
accepting the slightest obligation from him ; but in the present case and under the present circumstances I think it
would have been really false pride and apparently mischievous
affectation to have declined this mark of his Royal Highness's
confidence and favour."

It was no great return for so many services ; and even
this was not at first a satisfactory gift, since it had been
previously bestowed (hypothetically) on some one else,
and a long correspondence and many representations and
explanations seem to have been exchanged before Sheridan was secure in his post—the only profit he carried
with him out of his prolonged and brilliant political life.

The one instance, which has been referred to, in
which his political loyalty was defective occurred very
near the end of his career. Fox was dead, to whom,
though some misunderstanding had clouded their later
intercourse, he had always been faithful, and other leaders
had succeeded in the conduct of the party, leaders with
whom Sheridan had less friendship and sympathy, and
who had thwarted him in his wish to succeed Fox as the
representative of Westminster, an honour on which he had
set his heart. It was in favour of a young nobleman of no
account in the political world that the man who had so
long been an ornament to the party, and had in his day
done it such manful service, was put aside; and Sheridan
would have been more than mortal had he not felt it
deeply. The opportunity of avenging himself occurred
before long. When the Prince, his patron, finally came
to the position of Regent, under many restrictions, and
with an almost harsh insistence upon the fact that he
held the office not by right, but by the will of Parliament,
Sheridan had one moment of triumph—a triumph almost
whimsical in its completeness. In the ordinary course of
affairs it became the duty of the Lords Grey and Granville, the recognised leaders of the Whig party, which up
to this time had been the party specially attached to the
Prince, to prepare his reply to the address presented to
him by the Houses of Parliament: but the document,
when submitted to him, was not to the royal taste.
Sheridan, in the meanwhile, who knew all the thoughts
of his patron and how to please him, had prepared
privately, almost accidentally, according to his own account, a draft of another reply, which the Prince adopted
instead, to the astonishment and indignant dismay of

the official leaders, who could scarcely believe in the possibility of such an interference. Moore enters into a
lengthened explanation of Sheridan's motives and conduct, supported by his own letters and statements, of
which there are so many that it is very apparent he was
himself conscious of much necessity for explanation. The
great Whig Lords, who thus found themselves superseded,
made an indignant remonstrance; but the mischief was
done. In the point of view of party allegiance, the proceeding was indefensible; and yet we cannot but think
the reader will feel a certain sympathy with Sheridan in
this sudden turning of the tables upon the men who had
slighted him and ignored his claims. They were new
men, less experienced than himself, and the dangerous
gratification of showing that, in spite of all they might
do, he had still the power to forestal and defeat them,
must have been a very strong temptation. But such
gratifications are of a fatal kind. Sheridan himself, even
at the moment of enjoying it, must have been aware of
the perilous step he was taking. And it is another proof
of the curious mixture of capacity for business and labour
which existed in him along with the most reckless indolence and forgetfulness, that the literature of this incident
is so abundant; and that, what with drafts prepared for
the Prince's consideration, and letters and documents of
State corrected for his adoption, and all the explanatory
addresses on his own account which Sheridan thought
necessary, he was as fully employed at this crisis as if he
had been a Secretary of State.

This or anything like it he was not, however, fated to
be. A humbler appointment, that of Chief Secretary
under the Lord-Lieutenant of Ireland, had been designed

for him had the Whig party, as they anticipated, come
into office; although, after the mortification to which
Sheridan had subjected his noble chiefs, even such an
expedient of getting honourably rid of him might have
been more than their magnanimity was equal to.   But
these expectations faded as soon as the Regent was firmly
established in his place.   The Prince, as is well known,
pursued the course common to heirs on their accession,
and flung over the party of Opposition to which he had
previously attached himself.   The Whigs were left in
the lurch, and their political opponents continued in
power.   That Sheridan had a considerable share in
bringing this about seems evident: but in punishing
them he punished also himself.   If he could not serve
under them, it was evidently impossible that under the
other party he could with any regard to his own honour
serve.   There is an account in the anonymous biography
to which reference has been made, of an attempt on the
part of the Prince to induce Sheridan to follow himself
in his change of politics; but this has an apocryphal
aspect, as the report of a private conversation between
two persons, neither very likely to repeat it, always has.
It is added that, after Sheridan's refusal, he saw no more
of his royal patron.   Anyhow it would seem that the
intercourse between them failed after this point.   The
brilliant instrument had done its service, and was no
longer wanted.   To please his Prince, and perhaps to
avenge himself, he had broken his allegiance to his party,
and henceforward neither they whom he had thus deserted, nor he for whom he had deserted them, had any
place or occasion for him.   He continued to appear
fitfully in his place in Parliament for some time after,

and one of his latest speeches gives expression to his
views on the subject of Catholic Emancipation. Sheridan's nationality could be little more than nominal, yet
his interest in Irish affairs had always been great, and he
had invariably supported the cause of that troubled
country in all emergencies. In this speech, which was
one of the last expressions of his opinions on an Irish
subject, he maintains that the good treatment of the
Catholics was "essential to the safety of this empire."

"I will never give my vote to any administration that
opposes the question of Catholic Emancipation. I will not
consent to receive a furlough upon that particular question,
even though a ministry were carrying every other I wished.
In fine, I think the situation of Ireland a permanent consideration. If they were to be the last words I should ever
utter in this House, I should say, 'Be just to Ireland as you
value your own honour : be just to Ireland as you value your
own peace.'"

In this point at least he showed true discernment,
and was no false prophet.

The last stroke of evil fortune had, however, fallen
upon Sheridan several years before the conclusion of
his parliamentary life, putting what was in reality
the finishing touch to his many and long-continued
embarrassments. One evening in the early spring in
the year 1809 a sudden blaze illuminated the House
of Commons in the midst of a debate, lighting up the
assembly with so fiery and wild a light that the
discussion was interrupted in alarm. Sheridan was
present in his place, and when the intimation was made
that the blaze came from Drury Lane, and that his new
theatre, so lately opened and still scarcely completed,

o

was the fuel which fed this fire, it must have been a pale
countenance indeed upon which that fiery illumination
shone ; but he had never failed in courage, and this time
the thrill of desperation must have moved the man
whose ruin was thus accomplished. When some scared
member, perhaps with a tender thought for the orator
who had once in that place stood so high, proposed
the adjournment of the House, Sheridan, with the proud
calm which such a highly-strained nature is capable of
in great emergencies, was the first to oppose the impulse.
" Whatever might be the extent of the calamity," he
said, " he hoped it would not interfere with the public
business of the country." He left his brother members
to debate the war in Spain, while he went forth to
witness a catastrophe which made the further conduct of
any struggle in his own person an impossibility. Some
time later he was found seated in one of the coffee-houses
in Covent Garden " swallowing port by the tumblerful,"
as one witness says. One of the actors, who had been
looking on at the scene of destruction, made an indignant
and astonished outcry at sight of him, when Sheridan,
looking up with the wild gaiety of despair and that melancholy humour which so often lights up a brave man's
ruin, replied : " Surely a man may be allowed to take a
glass of wine by his own fireside." The blaze which
shone upon these melancholy potations consumed everything he had to look to in the world. He was still full
of power to enjoy, a man not old in years, and of the
temperament which never grows old : but he must have
seen everything that made life possible flying from him
in those thick coiling wreaths of smoke. There was
still his parliamentary life and his Prince's favour to fall

back upon, but probably in that dark hour his better judgment showed him that everything was lost.

After the moment of disaster, however, Sheridan's buoyant nature and that keen speculative faculty which would seem to have been so strong in him, awoke with all the fervour of the rebound from despair, as he began to see a new hope. In a letter addressed to Mr. Whitbread, written soon after the fire, and with the high compliment that he considered Whitbread "the man living in my estimation the most disposed and the most competent to bestow a portion of your time and ability to assist the call of friendship," he thus appeals to his kindness :—

"You said some time since, in my house, but in a careless conversation only, that you would be a member of a committee for rebuilding Drury Lane Theatre if it would serve me ; and indeed you very kindly suggested yourself that there were more persons to assist that object than I was aware of. I most thankfully accept the offer of your interference, and am convinced of the benefits your friendly exertions are competent to produce. I have worked the whole subject in my own mind, and see a clear way to retrieve a great property, at least to my son and his family, if my plan meets the support I hope it will appear to merit.

"Writing this to you in the sincerity of private friendship and the reliance I place on my opinion of your character, I need not ask of you, though eager and active in politics as you are, not to be severe in criticising my palpable neglect of all Parliamentary duty. It would not be easy to explain to you, or even to make you comprehend, or any one in prosperous and affluent plight, the private difficulties I have to struggle with. My mind and the resolute independence belonging to it has not been in the least subdued by the late calamity ; but the consequences arising from it have more engaged and embarrassed me than perhaps I have been willing to allow. It has been a principle of my life, persevered in through great difficulties, never to borrow money of a private friend : and this resolution I would starve rather than violate. When I ask you to take part in this settlement of my shattered affairs, I ask you only to do so after a previous investigation of every part of the past circumstances which relate to the truth. I wish you to accept in conjunction with those who wish to serve me, and to whom I think you would not object. I may be again seized with an illness as alarming as that I lately experienced. Assist me in relieving my mind from the greatest affliction that such a situation can again produce—the fear of others suffering by my death."

Sheridan's proposal was that the theatre should be rebuilt by subscription by a committee under the chairmanship of Whitbread, he himself and his son receiving from them an equivalent in money for their share of the property under the patent. This was done accordingly : Sheridan's share amounted to £24,000, while his son got the half of that sum. But the money which was to take the place of the income which Sheridan had so long drawn from the theatre, was, it is needless to say, utterly inadequate ; and was engulfed almost immediately by payments. Indeed the force of circumstances and his necessities compelled him to use it as he might have used a sum independent of his regular income which had fallen into his hand. Whitbread was not to be dealt with now as had been the world in general in Sheridan's brighter days. "He was perhaps," says Moore, "the only person whom Sheridan had ever found proof against his powers of persuasion ; " and as in the long labyrinth of engagements which Sheridan no more expected to be held closely to than he would himself have held to a bargain, he had undertaken to wait for his money until the theatre was rebuilt, there were endless controversies and struggles over every demand he made: and they were many.   Sheridan had pledged himself also to non-interference, to "have no concern or connection of any kind whatever with the new undertaking," with as little idea of being held to the pledge : and when his criticisms upon the plans, and attempts to alter them, were repulsed, and the promises he had made recalled to his memory, his indignation knew no bounds. "There cannot exist in England," he cries, "an individual so presumptuous or so void of common sense as not sincerely to solicit the aid of my practical experience on this occasion even were I not in justice to the subscribers bound to offer it." In short it is evident that he never had faced the position at all, but expected to remain to some extent at the head of affairs as of old, and with an inexhaustible treasury to draw upon, although he had formally renounced all claim upon either.   When he wrote indignantly to Whitbread as to an advance of £2000 which had been refused to him, and of which he declared that "this and this alone lost me my election" (to Stafford, whither he had returned after his failure at Westminster), Whitbread replied in a letter which paints the condition of the unfortunate man beset by creditors with the most pitiful distinctness.

"You will recollect the £5000 pledged to Peter Moore to answer demands : the certificates given to Giblet, Ker, Iremonger, Cross, and Hirdle, five each at your request : the engagements given to Ettes and myself, and the arrears to the Linley family.   All this taken into consideration will leave a large balance still payable to you.   Still there are upon that balance the claims upon you of Shaw, Taylor, and Grubb, for all of which you have offered to leave the whole of your compensation in my hand to abide the issue of arbitration."

Poor Sheridan! he had meant to eat his cake yet have it, as is so common.   In his wonderful life of shifts and chances he had managed to do so again and again. But the moment had come when it was no more practicable, and neither persuasion nor threats nor indignation could move the stern man of business to whom he had so lately appealed as the man of all others most likely to help and succour.   He was so deeply wounded by the management of the new building and all its arrangements that he would not permit his wife to accept the box which had been offered for her use by the committee, and it was a long time before he could be persuaded so much as to enter the theatre with which his whole life had been connected.   It was for the opening of this new Drury Lane that the competition of Opening Addresses was called for by the new proprietors, which has been made memorable by the "Rejected Addresses" of Horace and James Smith, one of the few burlesques which have taken a prominent place in literature.   It was a tradesman-like idea to propose such a competition to English poets, and the reader will willingly excuse the touch of bitterness in Sheridan's witty description of the Ode contributed by Whitbread himself, which, like most of the addresses, "turned chiefly on allusions to the Phœnix."   "But Whitbread made more of the bird than any of them," Sheridan said; "he entered into particulars and described its wings, beak, tail, etc.: in short it was a poulterer's description."

It was while he was involved in these painful controversies and struggles that Sheridan lost his seat in Parliament. This was the finishing blow. His person, so long as he was a member of Parliament, was at least

safe. He could not be arrested for debt; everything
else that could be done had been attempted, but this
last indignity was impossible. Now, however, that
safeguard was removed : and for this among other
reasons his exclusion from Parliament was to Sheridan
the end of all things. His *prestige* was gone, his power
over. It would seem to be certain that the Prince
of Wales offered to bring him in for a government
borough : but Sheridan had not fallen so low as that.
Once out of Parliament, however, the old lion was important to nobody. He could neither help to pass a
measure nor bring his eloquence to the task of smothering
one. He was powerless henceforward in State intrigues,
neither good to veil a prince's designs nor to aid a party
movement. And besides he was a poor broken-down
dissipated old man, a character meriting no respect, and
for whom pity itself took a disdainful tone. He had not
been less self-indulgent when the world vied in admiration and applause of him : but all his triumphs had now
passed away, and what had been but the gay excess of an
exuberant life became the disgraceful habit of a broken
man. His debts, which had been evaded and put out of
sight so often, sprang up around him no more to be
eluded. Once he was actually arrested and imprisoned
in a sponging-house for two or three days, a misery and
shame which fairly overcame the fortitude of the worn-
out and fallen spirit. "On his return home," Moore
tells us (some arrangements having been made by Whitbread for his release), "all his fortitude forsook him, and
he burst into a long and passionate fit of weeping at the
profanation, as he termed it, which his person had
suffered." Leigh Hunt, in his flashy and frothy article,

has some severe remarks upon this exhibition of feeling, but few people will wonder at it. Sheridan had been proud in his way, he had carried his head high. His own great gifts had won him a position almost unparalleled; he had been justified over and over again in the fond faith that by some happy chance, some half miraculous effort, his fortunes might still be righted and all go well. Alas! all this was over, hope and possibility were alike gone. Like a man running a desperate race, half stupefied in the rush of haste and weariness, of trembling limbs and panting bosom, whose final stumble overwhelms him with the passion of weakness, here was the point in which every horror culminated and every power broke down. The sanguine foolish bravery of the man was such even then, that next moment he was calculating upon the possibility of re-election for Westminster, a seat which was one of the prizes sought by favourites of fortune; and, writing to his solicitor after his personal possessions, pictures, books, and nicknacks had been sacrificed, comforted him with a cheerful "However, we shall come through!"

Poor Sheridan! the heart bleeds to contemplate him in all his desperate shifts, now maudlin in tears, now wild in foolish gaiety and hope. Prince and party alike left him to sink or swim as he pleased. When it was told him that young Byron, the new hero of society, had praised him as the writer of the best comedy, the best opera, the best oration of his time, the veteran burst into tears. A compliment now was an unwonted delight to one who had received the plaudits of two generations, and who had moved men's minds as few besides had been able to do. A little band of friends, very few and of no great renown, were steadfast to him, Peter Moore, M.P. for Coventry, Samuel Rogers, his physician Dr. Bain, he who had attended the deathbed of Mrs. Sheridan, stood by him faithfully through all; but he passed through the difficulties of his later years, and descended into the valley of the shadow of death, deserted, but for them, by all who had professed friendship for him. Lord Holland, indeed, is said to have visited him once, and the Duke of Kent wrote him a polite regretful letter when he announced his inability to attend a meeting; but not even an inquiry came from Carlton House, and all the statesmen whom he had offended, and those to whom he had long been so faithful a colleague, deserted him unanimously. When the troubles of his later life culminated in illness, a more forlorn being did not exist. He had worn out his excellent constitution with hard living and continual excesses. Oceans of potent port had exhausted his digestive organs; he had no longer either the elasticity of youth to endure, or its hopeful prospects to bear him up. He was, indeed, still cheerful, sanguine, full of plans and new ideas for "getting through," till the very end. But this had long been a matter beyond hope. His last days were harassed by all the miseries of poverty — nay, by what is worse, the miseries of indebtedness. That he should starve was impossible : but he had worse to bear, he had to encounter the importunities of creditors whom he could not pay, some at least of whom were perhaps as much to be pitied as himself. He was not safe night nor day from the assaults of the exasperated or despairing. "Writs and executions came in rapid succession, and bailiffs at length gained possession of his

house." That house was denuded of everything that
would sell in it, and the chamber in which he lay dying
was threatened, and in one instance at least invaded
by sheriffs' officers, who would have carried him off
wrapped in his blankets had not Dr. Bain interfered, and
warned them that his life was at stake. One evening
Rogers, on returning home late at night, found a despairing appeal on his table. "I find things settled so
that £150 will remove all difficulty; I am absolutely
undone and broken-hearted. I shall negotiate for the
plays successfully in the course of a week, when all
shall be returned. They are going to put the carpets
out of the window and break into Mrs. S.'s room and
take me. For God's sake let me see you." Moore was
with Rogers and vouches for this piteous demand on his
own authority. The two poets turned out after midnight to Sheridan's house, and spoke over the area rails
to a servant, who assured them that all was safe for the
night. Miserable crisis so often repeated! In the
morning the money was sent by the hands of Moore,
who gives this last description of the unfortunate and
forsaken—

"I found Mr. Sheridan good-natured and cordial, and
though he was then within a few weeks of his death, his
voice had not lost its fulness or strength, nor was that lustre
for which his eyes were so remarkable diminished. He
showed too his usual sanguineness of disposition in speaking
of the price he expected for his dramatic works, and of the
certainty he felt of being able to manage all his affairs if his
complaint would but suffer him to leave his bed."

Moore adds with natural indignation, that during the
whole of his lingering illness, "it does not appear that

any one of his noble or royal friends ever called at his
door, or even sent to inquire after him."

At last the end came. When the Bishop of London,
sent for by Mrs. Sheridan, came to visit the dying man,
she told Mr. Smyth that such a paleness of awe came
over his face as she could never forget. He had never
taken time or thought for the unseen, and the appearance of the priest, like a forerunner of death itself,
stunned and startled the man, whose life had been
occupied with far other subjects. But he was not one
to avoid any of the decent and becoming preliminaries
that custom had made indispensable—nay, there was so
much susceptibility to emotion in him, that no doubt he
was able to find comfort in the observances of a deathbed, even though his mind was little accustomed to reli-
gious thought or observance. Nothing more squalid,
more miserable and painful, than the state of his house
outside of the sick chamber could be. When Smyth arrived in loyal friendship and pity to see his old patron,
he found the desecrated place in possession of bailiffs, and
everything in the chill disorder which such a miserable
invasion produces. Poor Mrs. Sheridan, meeting him
with a kind of sprightly despair, suggested that he
must want food after his journey. "I daresay you
think there is nothing to be had in such a house ;
but we are not so bad as that," she cried. The
shocked and sympathetic visitor had little heart to
eat, as may be supposed, and he was profoundly moved
by the description of that pale awe with which Sheridan
had resigned himself to the immediate prospect of death.

In the meantime, some one outside, possibly Moore
himself, though he does not say so, had written a letter

to the *Morning Post*, calling attention to the utter desertion in which Sheridan had been left.

"Oh delay not," said the writer, without naming the
person to whom he alluded (we quote from Moore), " delay
not to draw aside the curtain within which that proud spirit
hides its sufferings." He then adds, with a striking antici-
pation of what afterwards happened, "Prefer ministering in
the chamber of sickness to mustering at

"The splendid sorrows that adorn the hearse.

"I say *life* and *succour* against Westminster Abbey and a
funeral. This article" (Moore continues) "produced a strong
and general impression, and was reprinted in the same paper
the following day."

So unusual a fact proves the interest which Sheridan
still called forth in the public mind. It had so much
effect that various high-sounding names were heard again
at Sheridan's door among the hangers-on of the law
and the disturbed and terrified servants, who did not
know when an attempt might be made upon their master's
person, dying or dead. The card even of the Duke of
York, the inquiries of peers or wealthy commoners, to
whom it would have been so easy to conjure all
Sheridan's assailants away, could no longer help or harm
him. After a period of unconsciousness, on a Sunday
in July, in the height of summer and sunshine, this
great ministrant to the amusement of the world, this
orator who had swayed them with his breath, died like
the holder of a besieged castle, safe only in the inmost
citadel, beset with eager foes all ready to rush in, and
faithful servants glad that he should hasten out of the
world and escape the last indignity. Among the many
lessons of the vicissitudes of life with which we are all

familiar, there never was any more effective. It is like
one of the strained effects of the stage, to which Sheridan's early reputation belonged; and like a curious
repetition of his early and sudden fame, or rather
like the scornful commentary upon it of some devilish
cynic permitted for the moment to scoff at mankind,
is the apotheosis of his conclusion. The man who
was hustled into his coffin to escape the touch which
he had dreaded so much in life, that profanation of
his person which had moved him to tears—and hastily
carried forth in the night to the shelter of his friend's
house that he might not be arrested, dead—was no
sooner covered with the funeral pall than dukes and
princes volunteered to bear it. Two royal highnesses,
half the dukes and earls and barons of the peerage,
followed him in the guise of mourning to Westminster
Abbey, where among the greatest names of English
literature, in the most solemn and splendid shrine
of national honour, this spendthrift of genius, this
prodigal of fame, was laid for the first time in all his
uneasy being to secure and certain rest. He had been
born in obscurity — he died in misery. Out of the
humblest unprovided unendowed poverty, he had blazed
into reputation, into all the results of great wealth, if
never to its substance; more wonderful still, he had risen
to public importance and splendour, and his name can
never be obliterated from the page of history ; but had
fallen again, down, down, into desertion, misery, and the
deepest degradation of a poverty for which there was
neither hope nor help : till death wiped out all possibilities
of further trouble or embarrassment, and Sheridan became
once more in his coffin the great man whom his party

delighted to honour—a national name and credit, one of
those whose glory illustrates our annals. It may be
permitted now to doubt whether these last mournful
honours were not more than his real services to England
deserved; but at the moment it was no doubt a fine
thing that the poor hopeless Sherry whom everybody admired and despised, whom no one but a few
faithful friends would risk the trouble of helping,
who had sunk away out of all knowledge into endless
debts, and duns, and drink, should rise in an instant as
soon as death had stilled his troubles into the Right
Honourable, brilliant, and splendid Sheridan, whose
enchanter's wand the stubborn Pitt had bowed under,
and the noble Burke acknowledged with enthusiasm.
It was a fine thing; but the finest thing was that death,
which in England makes all glory possible, and which
restores to the troublesome bankrupt, the unfortunate
prodigal, and all stray sons of fame, at one stroke,
their friends, their reputation, and the abundant tribute
which it might have been dangerous to afford them
living, but with which it is both safe and prudent to glorify
their tomb.   So Scotland did to Burns, letting him suffer
all the tortures of a proud spirit for want of a ten-pound
note, but sending a useless train of local gentry to attend
him to his grave—and so the Whig Peers and potentates
did to Sheridan, who had been their equal and companion.   Such things repeat themselves in the history of
the generations, but no one takes the lesson, though every
one comments upon it.   Men of letters have ceased, to
a great extent, to be improvident and spendthrifts, and
seldom require to be picked out of ruin by their
friends and disciples in these days; but who can doubt

that were there another Sheridan amongst us his fate
would be the same?

It has to be added, however, that had the great
people who did nothing for him stepped in to relieve
Sheridan and prolong his life, nothing is more prob-
able than that the process would have had to be repeated
from time to time, as was done for Lamartine in
France, since men do not learn economy, or the wise
use of their means, after a long life of reckless pro-
fusion. But he had gained nothing by his political
career, in which most of the politicians of the time
gained so much, and it is said that his liabilities came to
no more than £4000, for which sum surely it was not
meet to suffer such a man to be hunted to his grave by
clamorous creditors, however just their claim or natural
their exasperation. Somebody said in natural enthusiasm, when it was announced that the author of
Waverley was overwhelmed with debts, "Let every one
to whom he has given pleasure give him sixpence, and
he will be the richest man in Europe." Yes! but the
saying remained a very pretty piece of good nature and
pleasing appreciation, no one attempting to carry its
suggestion out. Sir Walter would have accepted no
public charity, but a public offering on such a grand
scale, had it ever been offered, would not have shamed
the proudest. These things are easy to say; the doing
only fails in our practical British race with a curious
consistency. It is well that every man should learn that
his own exertions are his only trust; but when that is
said it is not all that there should be to say.

"Where were they these royal and noble persons" (Moore
cries with natural fervour of indignation) "who now crowded

to 'partake the yoke' of Sheridan's glory ; where were they
all while any life remained in him ?   Where were they all
but a few weeks before when their interposition might have
saved his heart from breaking ? or when the zeal now
wasted on the grave might have soothed and comforted the
deathbed ? This is a subject on which it is difficult to speak
with patience.   If the man was unworthy of the commonest
offices of humanity while he lived, why all this parade of
regret and homage over his tomb ?"

And he adds the following verses which "appeared,"
he says, "at the time, and however intemperate in their
satire and careless in their style, came evidently warm
from the breast of the writer" (himself)—

" Oh, it sickens the heart to see bosoms so hollow,
    And friendships so false in the great and highborn ;
To think what a long line of titles may follow,
    The relics of him who died friendless and lorn.

" How proud they can press to the funeral array,
    Of him whom they shunned in his sickness and sorrow ;
How bailiffs may seize his last blanket to-day,
    Whose pall shall be held up by nobles to-morrow."

When all these details which move the heart out of
the composedness of criticism are put aside, we scarcely
feel ourselves in a position to echo the lavish praises
which have been showered upon Sheridan.   He was no
conscientious workman labouring his field, but an abrupt
and hasty wayfarer snatching at the golden apples where
they grew, and content with one violent abundance of
harvesting.   He had no sooner gained the highest successes which the theatre could give than he abandoned
that scene of triumph for a greater one ; and when—
on that more glorious stage—he had produced one of the

most striking sensations known to English political life, his interest in that also waned, and a broken occasional effort now and then only served to show what he might have accomplished had it been continuous. If he had been free of the vices that pulled him to earth, and possessed of the industry and persistency which were not in his nature, he would, with scarcely any doubt, have left both fortune and rank to his descendants. As it was in everything he did, he but scratched the soil. Those who believe that the conditions under which a man does his work, are those which are best adapted to his genius, will comfort themselves that there was nothing beyond this fertile surface, soon exhausted and capable of but one overflowing crop and no more, and there is a completeness and want of suggestion in his literary work which favours this idea. But the other features of his life are equally paradoxical and extraordinary; the remarkable financial operations which must have formed the foundation of his career were combined with the utmost practical deficiency in the same sphere; and his faculty for business, for negotiation, explanation, copious letter-writing, and statement of opinion, contrast as strangely with the absolute indolence which seems to have distinguished his life. He could conjure great sums of money out of nothing, out of vacancy, to buy his theatre, and set himself up in a lavish and prodigal life; but he could not keep his private affairs out of the most hopeless confusion. He could arrange the terms of a Regency and outwit a party; but he could not read, much less reply to, the letters addressed to him, or keep any sort of order in the private business on his hands. Finally, and perhaps most extraordinary of all, he could give in

P

the *Critic* the deathblow to false tragedy, then write the bombast of Rolla, and prepare *Pizarro* for the stage. Through all these contradictions Sheridan blazed and exploded from side to side in a reckless yet rigid course, like a gigantic and splendid piece of firework, his follies repeating themselves, his inability to follow up success, and careless abandonment of one way after another that might have led to a better and happier fortune. He had a fit of writing, a fit of oratory, but no impulse to keep him in either path long enough to make anything more than the dazzling but evanescent triumph of a day. His harvest was like a southern harvest, over early, while it was yet but May; but he sowed no seed for a second ingathering, nor was there any growth or richness left in the soon-exhausted soil.

Sheridan's death took place on the 7th July 1816, when he was nearly sixty-five, after more than thirty years of active political life. His boyish reputation, won before this began, has outlasted all that high place, extraordinary opportunity, and not less extraordinary success, could do for his name and fame.

THE END.

Printed by R. & R. CLARK, *Edinburgh.*